Creative Tucks and Textures

Galactic Star
75 × 75cm (30 × 30in)
Twelve Novel Variation
Trumpets (page 71) with
coloured fabric inserts.
Ruched centre embellished
with thread. Free-motion
machine quilting in metallic
thread. Created in batik – all
available from Hoffman of
California.
(Jennie Rayment)

Creative Tucks and Textures

For Quilts and Embroidery

JENNIE RAYMENT

B T BATSFORD

First published 2004

© Jennie Rayment 2004

The right of Jennie Rayment to be identified as Author of this work has been asserted by her in accordance with the Copyright, Designs and Patents Act 1988.

Volume © B T Batsford 2004

ISBN 0 7134 8913 8

A CIP catalogue record for this book is available from the British Library.

Photography by Michael Wicks

Printed in Malaysia
for the publishers
B T Batsford
The Chrysalis Building
Bramley Road
London W10 6SP

www.batsford.com

An imprint of Chrysalis Books Group

Acknowledgements

This book is dedicated to my mother – now she can have the all-colour singing and dancing proper book with my name down the spine resting on her coffee table!

Many, many thanks as ever have to be proffered to my valiant proofreaders. Patsy Yardley has once again come up trumps and worked her way through my excruciating grammar and punctuation. Dear Nick has yet again coughed, spluttered and waded his way through reams of paper. Shelagh Jarvis has read, checked and tried the various ideas, then made two fabulous quilts and a giant cushion. Harriet Pelham and Donna Sawyer (Virginia, USA) each created a delectable design to adorn the Gallery.

A special mention has to be included for the splendidly helpful editors at Batsford, particularly Nicola Birtwisle, who have all been brow-beaten into submission and forced to reproduce this verbal discourse. In addition, Michael Wicks has made the most supreme effort in flattening and flattering the samples and quilts in his superb photographs.

Last, but by no means least, I must thank my students who still suffer my teaching, lecturing and doubtless hectoring, and continue to return for more.

CONTENTS

INTRODUCTION

Creative Tucks and Textures is simply packed with information. Many different techniques, designs and amazing ways to manipulate material jostle for your attention. New and ingenious methods and machinations have been developed, and ideas from previous books have been extended in a wide variety of intriguing fabrications. Also included is a selection of interesting and inspiring projects plus a Gallery full of wonderful tactile and textured pieces of quilting and hangings.

Texture

Texture – the interplay of light and shadow – is an added dimension!

Rich colours and strong patterns have an immediate striking visual impact but texture adds depth and a 'touchy-feely' aspect to a surface. Many fabrics are textured initially – velvets have a deep soft pile; some silks have a silvery sheen with a smooth surface and some contain a random slub; twills and tweeds have a nubby and coarse-grained element arising from their woven design or the type of thread; the flat surface of polished and glazed cottons proffers an especially even gleam under a radiant source.

The addition of manipulation, stitch and other decorative embellishment enhances the natural characteristics of the fabric once the surface is illuminated. The material will change from a two-dimensional plane into a three-dimensional one, giving a new shape and form.

Texture is essential when using a monochromatic colour scheme to add visual interest. Pleasing optical variations will be created by the interchange of dark and light across manipulated or stitched areas. An otherwise dull and uninteresting surface will be brought to life when specific sections of the work are brought into relief and highlighted.

Playing with shape

Shape, form or pattern with a geometrical appearance has always pleased me, and the ideas in this book are mainly my own – a by-product of the fluff resting between my ears. The designs are often created by simply playing with pieces of material, paper, the napkin (when bored at a dinner party), the tablecloth (getting desperate), and anything else that comes to hand. Sometimes it is merely twiddling bits of material in a desultory fashion and suddenly an idea appears. Maybe a student makes an 'error' owing to misunderstanding a specific technique but, in adjusting the 'error', another creation arises. Once you begin to think in this fashion, then folds can be rolled, tucks twiddled or squashed and/or twisted, and pockets padded with or without an extra piece inserted.

Design inspiration

Look at all forms of sculpture from paper to chocolate, ancient and modern art, fashion through the ages, interior design and architecture for a wellspring for textured imagery. Plants, flowers, landscapes and natural formations contain a wealth of ideas. The juxtaposition, the optical dynamics, the harmonious interstructure (such wonderful expressions!) of your immediate surroundings cannot be dismissed as a fount of stimulation for constructive play.

This is a book for every age and level of skill from the novice to the complete expert. All kinds of textured and manipulated quilts, hangings, garments and soft furnishings can be created in any size or colour combination, with or without some sort of embroidered embellishment, and arranged in geometric or abstract and asymmetrical formations.

There is a wealth of creativity nestling between these pages. Twiddle, fiddle, nip, tuck, tweak, twitch, manipulate and manoeuvre as much as you like. None of the basic ideas is very difficult and, if the points don't meet in the more complicated structures, then buttons and beads are a girl or guy's best friend!

Textured Sampler
120 × 170cm (47 × 67in)
Inserted Rectangles with Trumpets; Interlocked Squares (clockwise); Double Bias Border; Crossed-Over Tucks; Tucks embellished with ribbon; Trumpets and Inserted Rectangles; Tucks embellished with thread; Interlocked Squares (anticlockwise); Trumpets and Inserted Triangles. Calico (muslin in USA) and batik material. Free-motion quilted.
Jennie Rayment

USEFUL INFORMATION

The boring bits!

'When in doubt read the destructions' is the normal modus operandi, so cast a glance over some of the suggestions regarding choice of fabrics, seams, borders and all kinds of other bits and pieces.

Choice of materials

Any fabric type can be used, but crisply finished materials with a firm weave are the easiest to manipulate and also hold their shape.

Medium-weight cotton, chintz (glazed cotton), cretonne and indeed calico (called muslin in the USA) or silk are ideal. Softer fibres (wool, voiles and gauze) and finely woven fabrics (thin silks and lawns) do not support texture well but are excellent if you desire a less defined effect. Thick materials such as velvets, corduroys, tweeds, felt and heavy linens are often too rigid to twist into intricate patterns, although by enlarging the selected textured design the result can be most effective.

Frequently, polyesters and other man-made fibres are too crease-resistant to hold any textured effect efficiently. Needless to say, some of the modern micropore fabrics look superb when textured, especially on a garment.

Washing fabrics
Quilts do require washing, albeit occasionally, so select an easily laundered fabric that retains its shape. Chintz looses its sheen and curtain lining resembles an old dishcloth, becoming very sad and floppy, when washed.

As some fabrics shrink and the coloured dyes may run, many people recommend prewashing of the fabric to remove these problems. This is an unmitigated nuisance but sensible.

Tip: *Wash in cool water (the creases don't set so easily), tumble dry or line dry until damp. Press well with either a steam or dry iron (depends on the amount of creasing). Spray starch to restore the 'body'. (Starch the material before cutting as the heat of the iron and the moisture from the starch may stretch and distort the pieces.)*

Colour and pattern selection
Plain and pale-coloured materials display the textured surface clearly and have good light-reflecting qualities. Chintz and lustrous silk respond well to texture; their inherent shine adds depth to the light and shade cast by the textured areas. Hand-dyes and very fine self-coloured prints are also a good choice. Darker and heavily patterned fabrics absorb more light and may conceal the finer details of an elaborate tucked or textured design. Oddly enough, black chintz is most effective, although the light source has to be correct for the full textural effects to be apparent.

Sewing machines

Any sewing machine will suffice, from a treadle to the latest high-tech computerized one. A swing-needle model with a range of patterns would be an advantage for decorative stitching, but hand embroidery could be substituted.

In addition to the regular presser foot, a ¼in foot, darning or hopper foot and an open-toe embroidery foot are the most useful. Cording, edge-stitching and pin-tucking feet may be helpful.

Measurement conversions

When using the techniques described in this book, work in either metric or imperial and not a mixture of the two. Not all the given imperial measurements are translated into their exact metric equivalent.

Seam allowance (S/A)

The usual S/A recommended in many patchwork and quilting books is 0.65/0.75cm (¼in). This is adequate for accurate piecing of points and joining of junctions when sewing two layers together.

In my opinion, a *1cm (⅜in) seam is preferable* when piecing multiple layers, as all the raw edges may not be accurately aligned. (With a bit of luck and fingers crossed, all layers will be caught in this larger seam.) Do not panic – working with a larger seam is not difficult. Use the standard presser foot and look on the throat plate (metal plate beneath): 1cm (⅜in) is often marked on the throat plate. Metric machines may have the plate printed in centimetres or millimetres; consequently 1cm will be displayed as 1 or 10 (10mm = 1cm). Imperial machines (often older models) frequently have their throat plates marked in eighths, thus ⅜in is easy to find.

Alternatively, move the needle from its central position towards the left-hand side of the presser foot (away from the main body of machine). On most models of machines the needle will now be 1cm (⅜in) away from the right-hand edge of the presser foot. (Many modern machines frequently have several needle positions – check which one is the most accurate.)

Failing all that, measure 1cm (⅜in) and rule a line on the fabric.

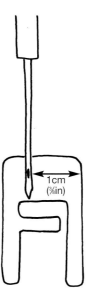

Stitch length and pressure

The pre-set (2/2.5mm) regular stitch length of many machines is fine for seaming two or three layers. Increase the stitch size slightly when sewing multiple layers, as the stitch size may contract owing to the feed dogs having difficulty in pulling many layers evenly.

On very thick or multilayered materials, slacken the pressure on the presser foot, by reducing the pressure – the fabrics can then be fed through more easily. To reduce the pressure, turn the dial/knob to a lower number/setting.

The pressure foot control dial/knob can be found – on the top of older models; inside the side cover (by light); underneath the lid on the left-hand side or outside the machine on the left-hand end. (If in doubt, refer to your instruction book – not all machines have this facility.)

Basting/tacking shapes

In Britain, the term 'tacking' normally refers to a series of long stitches (by hand or machine) temporarily holding layers in place. This interpretation is not universal. 'Tacking' in America means stitching all layers together firmly, as we would tack the carpet in place or pin a notice to the board. However, in most parts of the world, basting means a series of long stitches. To prevent any misunderstandings in this text, basting refers to a long stitch length.

Use the longest stitch length (highest number) on the machine and loosen the top tension slightly. This makes it easier to pull the threads out afterwards. Keep the basting close to the raw edges or wherever recommended in the instructions. Pin the layers carefully before commencing.

Sometimes the layers shift when the presser foot is lowered even when they are pinned thoroughly. To prevent this happening try the following tip.

- Lower the machine needle into one end of the shape/section before engaging the presser foot; by inserting the needle beforehand the layers of fabric are anchored and held firmly.

Starting the basting on the fabric with the presser foot and needle holding the layers firm will also help the feed dogs to guide the layers through more evenly.

Basting can always be done by hand if preferred.

Needle size

As a general rule, thin fabrics need a fine needle, e.g. 70 (10/11). Thicker fabrics or several layers require a fatter/larger, e.g. 90 (14), needle to allow the machine to pierce through the increased depth of fibres. (The higher the number, the larger the needle.)

Thread saver

An invaluable device that saves yards and yards of thread. It is really a method of *continuous sewing*, rather like chain piecing in patchwork. (This is not my own idea – it's an old tailoring trick.)

- Rummage in the trash bin and find a small scrap of unwanted fabric.

- At the end of any line of stitching, do not lift the presser foot, do not remove the work or cut the threads but continue to sew. Sew off the work onto this scrap of material and stop on the scrap. The presser foot is now sitting on the scrap of material. Leave the scrap there – do not move it.

- Detach the work from the small scrap by cutting the threads immediately behind (at the back of) the presser foot (between scrap and work).

- Continue with the next set of seams/piecing. Sew off the scrap and down the next seam (scrap is now attached to the start of the work). At the end of this line of stitching, cut the scrap off from the start and sew from the main piece of work onto the scrap once again. Cut threads behind the presser foot. Repeat, repeat, repeat, etc.!

This scrap is called a thread saver and will save a vast amount of thread – no long dangling ends; it prevents tangled threads at the start of the seam; threads snag less often in the bottom bobbin; the needle does not unthread inadvertently because the threads were cut too short, and it's energy-saving – no need to raise the presser foot. Finally, for those who habitually deviate at the end of a seam, it may help to keep you on the straight and narrow.

Give the idea a go – it seems complicated but is very easy when you get the hang of it.

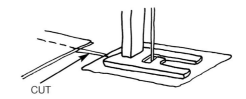

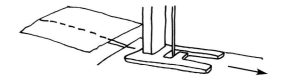

Remember: the only place to cut the threads is behind the presser foot (once you have sewn on to the thread saver and have stopped).

'Blind hem' stitch

This stitch is frequently used for securing the edge of a design or shape and, when employed carefully, gives the appearance of very neat hand stitching. Everyone is amazed at your 'hand sewing skills', yet it was machined – it's a fake!

The best blind hem stitch pattern consists of a bite (indent) with four to five straight stitches in between. Many machines do this particular stitch but some machines have a variation that would suffice.

Set the machine: stitch width 1, stitch length 1.

- For current Husqvarna Viking machines try stitch width 1.5, stitch length 0.4. Designer 1 & 2 owners: stitch width 1, stitch length 0.3.

- Some of the later Pfaff models appear to reduce the stitch width to 2 only. Try this trick: Press twin needle button; when it is activated (light on), the stitch width is reduced by 2. Consequently if you set stitch width at 3, press the twin needle setting button – the stitch width will now be 1. (This is a good technique for reducing the width of many patterns but it doesn't apply to all Pfaff models.)

- The LCD display on some makes of machine shows the correct settings (1 stitch width and length) but in reality the stitch is wider. These particular models cannot reduce the stitch width below a certain measurement because of some special internal override.

Having adjusted the stitch to the desired setting, carefully sew round the edge of the rolled fold. Keep the straight stitching very close to the outside of the fold and just catch the edge of the fold with the fine 'bite' (indent). Practise first!

An 'open-toed' presser foot gives a clearer view of the edge of the fold than the regular presser foot.

Open-toed feet for most models are available from your dealer. Alternatively, create one by snapping the central bar out of the Perspex appliqué foot. Do not use the designated blind hem foot (if one is supplied) – you are not making a blind hem but using the stitch as a method of appliqué.

Invisible or nylon filament is ideal, although a thread well matched to the appliquéd fabric will suffice. The top tension on the machine should be reduced (lower number) when you are using nylon filament. Fill the bottom bobbin with cotton thread (for preference), not nylon.

Pressing seams

Pressing all the layers to the same side makes one half of the seam very bulky, although the seam junction is supposedly stronger as one layer covers the join. Sometimes this is the best option, or it may be recommended for fast piecing in certain types of patchwork, e.g. strip patchwork. For a more evenly spread seam, press open and flat.

Before deciding whether the seam is pressed open or to one side, look inside the seam – is there some helpful information re points/junctions?

Open seams are informative

Depending on the type of piecing, a small 'V' or maybe a triangle of a different colour may be apparent on the wrong side (W/S). The base of this mark is the top of the point on the right side (R/S).

Technically the distance from the base of the mark to the raw edge should be the seam allowance, but if there are inaccuracies this might be different!

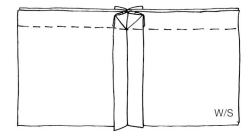

The next line of stitch must pass exactly through the base of the 'V' or triangle for accurate piecing.

Borders

Measuring borders on quilts

Measure the width/length of the quilt across the centre or at least several centimetres/inches away from the outside edge. The outside edges sometimes stretch resulting in inaccurate measurements.

Bordering square blocks/quilts

This natty technique needs four strips the same length.

To calculate the length:

1. Measure the block; deduct the seam allowance to get the finished measurement. (This is the measurement after the outside edge has been seamed.)

2. Decide on the finished width of the border.

The length of the strips is the finished width/length of the block (1) plus the finished width of the border (2) *plus seam allowances*.

Therefore a 30cm (12in) block with a 7.5cm (3in) border requires four strips of 37.5 × 7.5cm (15 × 3in) plus relevant seam allowances.

● Line up the first strip *with the lower edge* of the block. Start the sewing approximately 5cm (2in) from top of the block leaving several centimetres/inches of the border strip unattached. Sew to the bottom.

● Open out and attach the remaining strips. Each strip should fit exactly – if not, check your mathematics! Complete the stitching by turning the block over and finishing the first seam.

Pieced borders

Stitching identical blocks together to make a border can have difficulties: The length of the border is not divisible by the size of the block, i.e. six sections fit but seven do not.

Solve the problem by including another piece of material to redress the balance. Insert the extra piece in the centre of the border or divide in two and attach it to the ends. The extra section could be a contrasting colour or a different design, or include some appliqué. Be inventive (no one needs know that the border did not quite fit).

Positioning borders accurately

Sometimes it is necessary to move a border inward, setting it at a greater distance from the edge than the predetermined seam allowance.

Ruling a guideline at the designated seam allowance parallel to the desired stitching line solves the problem. The raw edge of the border is butted to the drawn line and, when the designated S/A is sewn, the stitching will now pass through the selected point. Trim the edges when the stitching is completed.

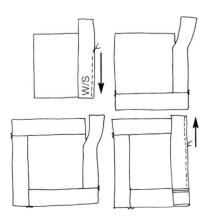

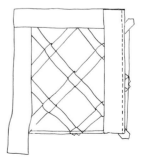

Favourite sewing gadgets

If you are ever stuck on a desert island, flower pins and wooden barbecue sticks would be most desirable, in addition to the sewing machines, fabric stash, rotary cutter, etc.

Flower pins score highly because they are extremely sharp and long, and have a flat head. They pass easily through many layers and, when you are ruling or cutting, the heads lie happily under a ruler, *but* the flower ends tend to fall off leaving a fairly useless pin and it is possible to sew through the heads on the machine. Overall the pros outweigh the cons in my opinion, so treat yourself to some. Just be careful to buy the right sort as one type of these pins is not as fine, more like a poker. Ask before you purchase.

Wooden barbecue sticks are an absolute must. They are ideal for holding the layers together as they are fed through under the presser foot; pushing recalcitrant corners under while you are

stitching; poking points out (use the blunt end) and scoring guidelines on material. These can be obtained from most hardware and ironmongers stores and many supermarkets. The best size is 15cm (6in) as the much longer 25cm (10in) ones are a little unwieldy, but you can snap the end off to reduce the size. The 15cm (6in) ones fit nicely in the hand.

Two rubber door props are good for tilting the machine. If the back edge of the machine is tilted up while you are sewing, the strain on your shoulders is reduced and the overall view of the working surface greatly improved.

Chalk markers are the last 'must have'. They are excellent for marking dark fabrics and drawing lines for machine quilting. Take a little care as the chalk residue does rub off easily.

Read this whole chapter before commencing any technique.

Barbecue sticks and flower pins.

Tucked Quilt
138 × 138cm (54 × 54in)
Nine identical tucked panels
with 5cm (2in) sashing.
Tucked border. Created in
medium-weight calico
(muslin in USA) on polyester
wadding with calico
backing. Machine pieced
and quilted.
Jennie Rayment

TUCKS

Tucks and pleats in one form or another have been used for centuries, mainly as ornamentation on clothing and more recently in soft furnishings. Old sewing manuals state that a tuck was a stitched fold: the fabric was creased firmly then stitched by hand. Nowadays, a machine speeds the process.

Pleats are different. They are not stitched along the length but merely folded over and sewn at one or both ends.

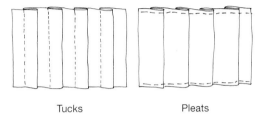

Tucks   Pleats

With the advent of the sewing machine, panels of tucks were frequently inserted into garments for decoration. Shirts and bodices had vertical or horizontal tucks down the front either longitudinally or horizontally. Groups of fine tucks embellished jabots, babies' gowns and crêpe de Chine handkerchiefs. These tucks were usually left flat (untwisted).

Gradually, the sewing fraternity developed more attachments and techniques for specialized sewing effects on the machine. For example, the combination of a twin needle, a particular type of presser foot and two reels of thread were used to make very fine tucks usually referred to as pin tucks (supposedly the width of a pin).

Eventually, a helpful tool called the 'Pleater' was invented to save some of the labour in folding a series of pleats. This ingenious gadget enabled the machine to pleat as it sewed: a single strip of fabric fed into the 'Pleater' was automatically folded into pleats before being stitched. In addition, the size and spacing of the pleats could be altered by moving one of the levers on the machine. These intriguing machines are still available and not only pleat but also can be set for gathering.

Other devices have been produced to make tucking procedures easier, such as the 'Perfect Pleater'. This natty invention is composed of several thin sheets of cardboard, which are carefully layered and glued together. Fabric is pushed into the space beneath each sheet then a piece of iron-on interfacing pressed on top. A series of accurately sized pleats is created without any need for sewing. The addition of the interfacing stabilizes the material but hinders much creative development.

By making individually sewn tucks, the possibilities for creative play, inventive manipulation and experimental embellishment are enormous.

One of the pleating devices for sewing machines.

Pin Tuck Panel
54 × 50cm (21 × 20in)
Spiral Log Cabin made from
pin-tucked and plain strips.
Twisted tucks on border.
Jennie Rayment

Making Tucks

Choice of fabrics

A crisply finished, medium-weight material in a plain colour or a simple self-patterned print is ideal. Cottons, silks and other natural fibres are preferable to man-made fibres such as polycottons. Heavily decorated or large multicoloured designs tend to obscure the textured effect.

Use spray starch before cutting fabric to add 'body' to a limp, soft or fine material. Stiffer materials usually crease better and support the texture more efficiently than soft ones.

Accuracy of stitching

Many people worry about the precision of their seams, piecing techniques and the junctions of the 'points'. Pleasingly, when making tucks, minor aberrations are concealed in the textured surface. The interplay of light and shadow hides a multitude of sins, so mistakes do not matter – the result is just a little different!

Direction of grain

Sewing tucks parallel to the warp threads then twisting across the weft is a good way to begin. This minimizes distortion.

Warp threads run from one end of the fabric to the other and are tighter than the weft threads, which lie across the material (from selvedge to selvedge). As the weft 'gives' more than the warp it has a greater flexibility, and tucks will twist more easily.

The warp and weft are easily discerned if the selvedge is visible: the warp threads are parallel to the selvedge. If not apparent, try pulling the fabric: it will stretch more along the weft grain.

Alternatively, grasp a short section of the fabric firmly, give a sharp tug and listen to the noise; warp threads produce a higher note than the weft. This is rather like a drum skin:

- looser skin – lower note = (stretchier) weft

- tighter skin – higher note = (tauter) warp

Washing and pressing

Hand wash the finished item in warm water, roll up in a towel and gently squeeze out any excess moisture. Tumble-drying for a short period is best, but remove the article while it is still slightly damp. Press lightly, using the point of the iron to ease the tucks back in place.

Making a panel of Tucks

1. Cut a wide strip of fabric, and remove the selvedges. On the Right Side (R/S), draw small neat and clearly visible marks (use a pencil/chalk/fabric marker) along both long edges at 2.5cm (1in) intervals. Mark one edge first then mark the opposite one – both sets of marks on either edge should be aligned. *Do not rule lines across the fabric.* Thread top and bottom spool of the sewing machine with thread to match the material.

2. Fold fabric on the first set of marks (pencil mark on the edge of fold). Using a normal stitch length (approximately 2.5), sew from edge to edge about 0.75cm (¼in) from the fold. The seam need not be precisely this measurement but *should be consistent.* Try to sew a parallel seam to the fold, and use a thread saver (page 10).

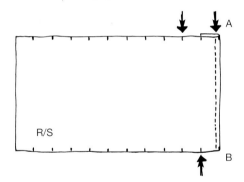

3. Having made the first tuck, turn the work round and refold the fabric on the next set of marks. Sew the next seam, taking care not to catch the outer edge of the material in the second tuck. Repeat the folding and stitching on every set of marks. Turn the work each time, sewing each seam in the opposite direction to the previous one, as this helps to prevent the tucked fabric distorting.

Tip: *When lines of stitch are constantly sewn in the same direction, i.e. top **A** to bottom **B,** the presser foot drags the fibres slightly each time, consequently pulling the material out of shape. By commencing sewing from **A** towards **B,** turning work and sewing the next seam from **B** to **A,** the fibres will be less distorted.*

As the work is turned, on every other seam the tucks will be underneath.

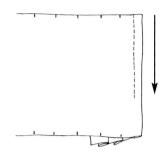

4. Continue until all the tucks are made or boredom sets in! Press all the tucks firmly in the same direction; press both the tucked (right) side and the reverse (wrong) side well. Do not worry if the seam lines on the reverse appear to be uneven; once the tucks have been manipulated any little meandering or deviation in the seaming will be concealed.

5. Stitch all the tucks down in the same direction along one edge.

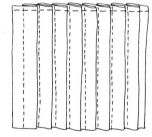

6. Turn the work and sew a second line parallel to the first line, twisting the tucks over as you go (tucks lie in opposite direction). The distance between these two lines of stitch is your choice. If the second line of stitch is too close to the first then the tucks will not lie absolutely flat and the fabric may distort. Does it matter? Why not experiment?

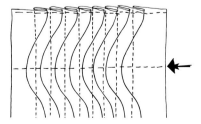

7. Complete the panel with parallel lines of stitching (equally or randomly spaced; the decision is yours), finishing on the outer edge. Lines of stitch spaced approximately 5–6.5cm (2–2½in) apart will create an interesting texture and not distort the finished sample too much.

8. Keep the stitching straight by ruling guidelines, lightly marking the edge of the tucks (this will be hidden when the tucks are twisted over). Mark one line at a time to avoid confusion – as the tucks twist, on alternate rows the tucks need to be marked on the opposite side.

Tip: *Use a small wooden barbecue/kebab skewer or point of stitch ripper or small fine scissors to help turn the tuck and hold it down while sewing. Fingers are not always nimble enough to hold the fabric precisely where needed, and a machine needle through the finger is best avoided. Alternatively, attach the quilting guide for speed and reasonable accuracy.*

Quilting guides
Quilting guides are extremely useful bits of equipment. Some machines have a quilting guide in their attachments box, but they are available for most models and not expensive.

1. Screw/attach/slot the guide into the presser foot (most guides fit on the *right-hand* side of presser foot). Set the guide at the desired distance (measuring from the edge of the guide to the needle).

2. Sew the first row; place the edge of the guide on this stitched line and sew the second one. *The edge of the quilting guide must follow the first line of stitch exactly.*

3. As the guide operates on one side of the presser foot (very few machines have right and left-hand guides), the fabric may distort because the work has to be sewn in the same direction each time. To overcome this problem sew the first line across the centre of the tucked panel; sew one half working from the centre line out, turn work round then sew the

other half (also working from the centre out). As one half of the sample is pulled one way and the other half in the opposite direction, the tucked panel should remain fairly straight. If any distortion occurs then straighten the fabric with a good tug and/or press heavily in the opposite direction.

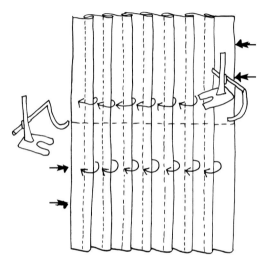

Quilting guide follows line of stitch. Wooden stick holds tuck in place before stitching.

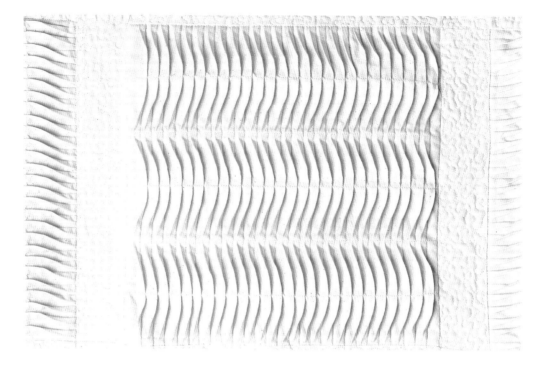

*Detail of **Tucked Quilt** (page 14).*

A tucked quilt block

Finished size: 30 × 30cm (12 × 12in)
Seam allowance (S/A): 0.75cm (¼in)

1. Cut a strip of fabric 31.5 × 71cm (12½ × 28in) approximately (this measurement allows for slight discrepancies in size of tucks).

2. Measure and mark 3cm (1¼in) from one end. Mark the remainder of both long edges at 2.5cm (1in) intervals, leaving about a 3cm (1¼in) space at the other end. In addition, mark *lightly* across the centre at the same measurements.

3. Complete about twenty tucks then check the measurement of the strip; pull gently before measuring as the work will stretch a little. Continue making tucks until the tucked fabric panel measures approximately 31.5cm (12½in) wide, including a 3cm (1¼in) space at both ends. Press well.

4. Sew along one edge of the tucks leaving a 0.75cm (¼in) S/A, and stitching all the tucks in one direction.

5   Measure and mark the rest of the fabric at 5cm (2in) intervals. Sew back and forth,

twisting the tucks as you go, working down the material. Finally sew a 0.75cm (¼in) seam on the bottom edge.

Why not use the quilting guide for speed and ease of measuring?

1. Sew across the centre of the panel then set guide at 5cm (2in).

2   Sew two rows either side of the centre before stitching along the outer edges.

3. Sew the outside lines on the seam allowance.

More ideas

*   The tucks could be left flat then twisted and stitched in place at the quilting stage. Sewing the tucks down through a layer of wadding and backing fabric will enhance the textural effect, as deeper shadows will form where the lines of stitch lie. (Use a walking foot or a darning/hopper foot to prevent the layers of fabric and wadding creeping unevenly.)

*   Sew several panels together to form a small quilt or hanging – adding a border between the panels solves the problem of matching the individual tucks. This border could be quilted in some fashion.

Designing with Tucks

Any length or width of fabric can be tucked. To calculate how much fabric to cut, decide on the size of the tuck. A rough estimate can be made: one 0.75cm (¼in) tuck takes up 1.5cm (½in) of material; therefore for every 2.5cm (1in) interval along the width, the fabric shrinks by 1.5cm (½in).

Err on the side of 'more is better'! A minor discrepancy in seam width can make a big difference. It is easier to cut off any excess material than to add on.

Change the distance between the Tucks

Increase or decrease the distance between the tucks. Measuring whole centimetres or inches is not difficult, but adding multiples of odd decimals or fractions such as 4.1cm (1⅝in) can be awkward.

Solve this problem by cutting a strip of card to the desired measurement and using this instead of a ruler. At all times, use a sharp pencil held at 45° to the edge of the card.

Joining two sections together

1. Construct the tucks on both pieces first, and press in the same direction.

2. Leave one set of marks either side of the proposed join unsewn.

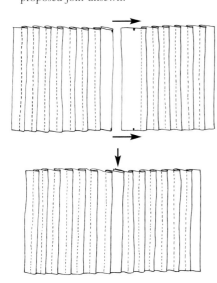

3. Fold the first piece of fabric along these marks and lay it on top of the second one – the distance between the individual tucks and this fold should be the same.

4. Sew down the folded edge using the same seam allowance as the rest of the tucks. Press.

Making long tucked panels

Add an extra set of measurements every 15–20cm (6–8in) or thereabouts down the length. Mark lightly. Check that each tuck is folded through the correct set of marks. Pressing then pinning each tuck before sewing is a good idea.

Experimental ideas

Change the sizes of the Tucks

- Create deeper areas of shadow with wider tucks or make narrower tucks for a gently corrugated effect. The width of the tucks can be altered easily by moving the needle over – nearer to or further from the inner edge of the presser foot. The lines on the throat plate are also useful as a seam guide.

- Very narrow tucks (similar to pin tucks) can be made with the zipper foot. Use the edge of the zipper foot as a guide, and check the needle is in the correct place before you commence sewing.

- Explore the effect of different sizes of tucks: alternate wide tucks with narrow ones. Wider tucks create more shadows but narrower ones appear to ripple across the material. Try two wide and two narrow tucks. (If the tucks are really wide then omit the next set of marks. There is no reason why a tuck has to be made on every set of marks.)

Change the measurements

- Mark the long edges at 5cm (2in) intervals to make larger tucks.

- Do all the markings have to be consistent – what about random measurements? Keep the tucks parallel by marking identical intervals on the opposite edge.

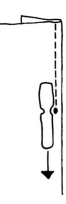

- When twisting the tucks, how about altering the distance between the lines of stitching? The rows do not have to be the same distance apart: play, and experiment. Leave part of the fabric flat (untwisted): this could be embellished afterwards.

Forget about accuracy and measuring

- Fold the fabric; sew a tuck any size and in any direction, completely at random – think of craggy rocks and the lines in crazy paving. Leave the tucks untwisted.

- Why not stitch the tucks down with an irregular curved line? Great idea for all those who can't sew straight – just wiggle across the material (see photograph on page 23)! Look at the ripples on the beach, rock strata or tree bark for design inspiration.

Directional materials

Striped fabrics lend themselves to tucking, as no marking is required. Check that the stripes are relatively straight before starting – not all striped designs are totally parallel.

Tucked striped material.

Preventing distortion of a tucked panel

- Place a tucked but not twisted panel onto some thin wadding/batting, and pin the layers together. Twist the tucks and sew in place through both layers to add stability and minimize distortion.

Embellishing the Tucks

Decorate with machine stitching

- Use a patterned stitch to secure the twisted tucks and/or stitch between the rows of tucks before twisting. (The tucks could be sewn initially with an 'invisible' thread (nylon filament). This will be concealed when sewn over with the decorative design.) Test the stitch design first, as some intricate patterns do not reproduce accurately on uneven surfaces.

- How about satin-stitching down the edge of a tuck with a variegated thread before twisting?

Appliqué over stitching

- Conceal the stitching of the twisted tucks with a ribbon, braid, textured wool or a thick decorative thread (see photograph on page 6).

Appliqué before twisting

After pressing (before any other stitching), appliqué a thin ribbon, braid or embroidery thread to the edge of some or all of the tucks.

1. Fill the top and bottom spool with the same colour as the appliqué. For those who prefer nylon filament (invisible thread) thread *top or bottom spool* with this and use ordinary thread on the other. Do not use invisible thread on both spools, as the machine may not sew properly.

2. Lay the thread alongside the tuck, and attach it to the fold of the material with a fairly fine and narrow zigzag. The width of the zigzag has to be just wide enough to cover the attached thread and sew into the edge of the tucked material.

3. Keep the thread on the very edge of the tuck, and sew up one tuck and down the other to prevent distortion. On occasions it may be more efficient to work in the same direction – realign the material with a good tug if it distorts.

4. If parts of the appliqué are not caught, restitch where necessary. Commence with a few very short straight stitches into the applied fibre then increase stitch width and length to the previous settings. Cover the faulty section, and complete the sewing with a few very short straight stitches. Trim thread ends. (Beginning or ending a seam with very small stitches prevents the stitching from unravelling when it is trimmed.)

Decorate with paint

● Using a contrasting-coloured fabric paint, lightly brush the edges of the tucks.

More ideas

● Sew tucks down by hand, adding beads or buttons, and/or embellish with French knots, etc.

● Carry an embroidery thread from one part of the stitching to another, creating a series of decorative loops. This can be done on the machine using the darning foot. (This is not suitable for frequently handled items, as fingers can catch in the loops.)

Make a wide band of Tucks

● Cut into squares and strips then use these for a creative interpretation of a patchwork design.

Assorted panels of tucks: wide and narrow tucks, honeycomb design, wiggly and straight stitched tucks, embellished with buttons and applied threads; six 60° triangles stitched to form a hexagon. All samples constructed from calico (muslin in USA).

- Cut into four equal strips and use for a border (see photograph on page 66).

- Cut into equilateral (60°) triangles and sew together to form a hexagon.

- Cut squares of tucked fabric. Sew together then twist the tucks on the diagonal.

Just play – you are the artist and nothing is wrong. It is just a little different!

Tip: *If you can't sew straight then wiggle across the tucks. A most excellent solution to the morning wobbles after a heavy evening down at the local hostelry!*

Wiggly Tucks
42 × 47cm (16½ × 18½in)

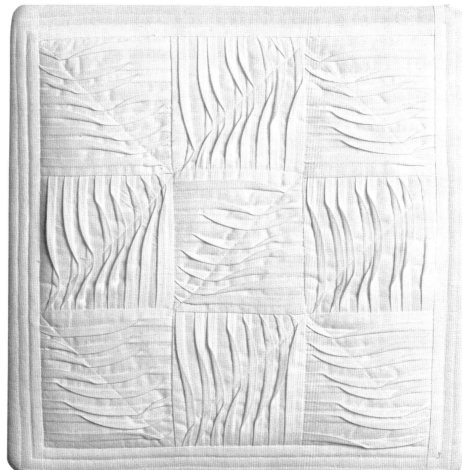

Diagonal Twisted Tucked Panel
*35 × 35cm (14 × 14in)
Nine squares of tucked fabric stitched together then twisted and sewn across the diagonal.*

*Both these panels were constructed from medium-weight calico (muslin in USA).
Jennie Rayment*

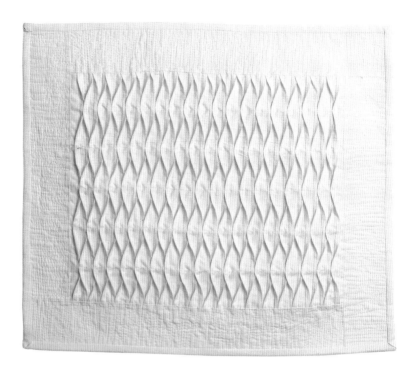

*Honeycomb Twisted
Tucked Panel*
53 × 45cm (21 × 17¾in)
*All calico on polyester
wadding. Free-motion
quilted border.*
Jennie Rayment

Twisting Tucks in 'honeycomb' patterns

Turning all the tucks in the same direction can become monotonous – why not alternate the twist and create a more ingenious design?

1. Construct an even number of tucks, i.e. pairs of tucks, and press them all in the same direction. As you sew along the edge twist one of each pair towards the other one so that they touch or overlap. Repeat with the next pair and so on, until every pair of tucks is turned towards each other.

2. Turn the work round and sew back across the tucks, reversing the procedure so that each tuck twists in the opposite direction. The distance between these two lines of stitch is your choice. This pattern is repeated until the entire section is tucked.

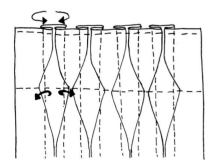

To some people this seems easy to understand, but others can puzzle over the description. Here is an alternative explanation.

1. Make an even number of tucks (i.e. divisible by two). You will now have pairs of tucks, or let's call them couples of tucks. A very common couple that we all understand is Mummy and Daddy: divide the tucks into sets of Mummies and Daddies.

2. As you sew down the edge of the tucked panel, twist each Mummy so that she 'kisses' each Daddy (marital harmony). You may well find that Mummy actually puts her arms around Daddy (tucks overlap), it makes for real lovey-doveyness!

3. However, when it comes to sewing the next row, our happy couples have an enormous argument and turn away from each other. Now, as you sew the second line of stitch, Mummy kisses the Daddy from next door! Will divorce be the next step?

4. Fortunately, when it comes to the third row, all our unhappy couples make it up and Mummy kisses Daddy again as on the first line. This pattern of marital harmony and divorce continues all the way down the material.

Why not extend the idea and have two tucks turning one way and two tucks the other or go one further and have two pairs of tucks with a small one in between? The mind boggles!

For even more ornamentation, before or after twisting the tucks, add some embellishment as described on page 21.

Twice-Tucked and Twisted designs

How about tucking the work from top to bottom and then from side to side? This produces a tucked grid, which has all manner of exciting possibilities for design development. It's neat and nifty, tactile and textural!

This particular pattern consists of a row of evenly seamed tucks made from one side of the fabric to the other (vertically). These are pressed flat and a further set made across the first ones (horizontally). As the horizontal tucks are sewn, the vertical tucks are twisted in alternating directions creating a criss-crossed grid.

Making a 45cm (18in) approx. finished panel

1. Cut one 62cm (25in) square.

2. Make a small, distinct pencil mark on the top edge, 6cm (2½in) from one corner. Make ten further marks at 5cm (2in) intervals, leaving a 6cm (2½in) space at the other side. Repeat these marks at the same spacing every 12cm (5in) down the fabric, finishing on the lower edge. (Fabric is now marked vertically.)

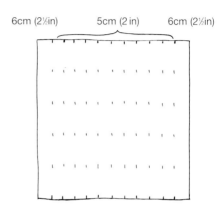

6cm (2½in) 5cm (2 in) 6cm (2½in)

3. Fold the fabric on the first set of vertical marks, ensuring that all the marks are precisely on the edge of the fold. Pin the fold if necessary, and sew a 0.75cm (¼in) seam. The first tuck is now made. Repeat on the next ten sets of marks to make 11 tucks in total. Ideally, each tuck should be sewn in the opposite direction to prevent the material distorting. Use a Thread Saver (see page 10).

4. On the R/S, press all the tucks in the same direction. Turn the fabric over and press on the W/S gently to make sure that the material is lying flat; sometimes the fabric 'catches' in the underside of the seam.

Denim & Stripes
72 × 48cm (28½ × 19in)
Tucked and twisted design with free-motion quilted border on polyester wadding.
Jennie Rayment

5. Mark the other sides at the same intervals as described before – leave 6cm (2½in) at beginning, mark remainder at 5cm (2in) intervals, etc. Mark each tuck or rule very faint lines across the material. (A chalk marker is ideal for this.)

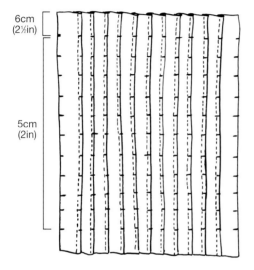

6cm (2½in)

5cm (2in)

6. Fold the material on the first set of lines and sew the first tuck across the previous ones. Before sewing the next tuck across the material, twist the original tucks over and *pin them down*. Repeat on each set of marks, reversing the twist of the tuck each time. Pinning is essential! Try to remember to alternate the direction of the stitching to prevent distortion. If the tucks are not absolutely accurate – panic not. Remember that texture creates areas of light and shade, so with a bit of luck any aberrations in the sewing will be disguised in the shadows. Mistakes may not matter quite so much!

7. Secure each intersection of the tucks with a few stitches to retain the twisted effect: use a very small stitch length or put the darning/hopper foot on the machine; 'jump' from one intersection to the other and cut all the threads afterwards on both sides of the material. For more ornamentation, use a decorative pattern with a contrasting-coloured thread to the fabric.

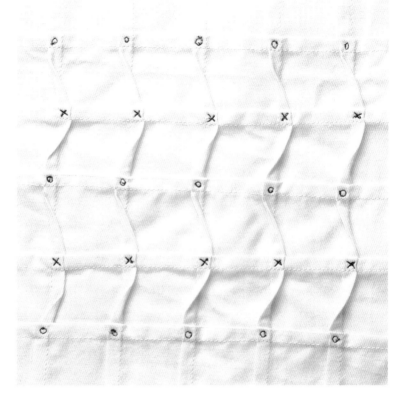

8. Finally, stitch round the outer edge and twist each tuck over as you sew (see photograph on page 27). Complete the design by sewing along the outer edge of the material to secure the tucks, twisting them as you stitch (see photograph on page 27).

Stage 6: Horizontal tuck sewn across material with initial (vertical) tucks twisted over and pinned down.

Intersections secured with decorative pattern and contrasting thread.

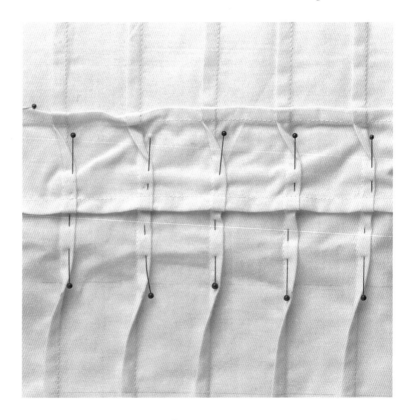

Bias Twice-Tucked and Twisted design with decorative stitching.

by the second set of tucks crossing over the first.

- Try the **Twice-Tucked technique on the bias**. Measure and mark the fabric on all four sides at 7cm (2⅞in) intervals (*not* 5cm [2in]). Sew the first set of tucks on the diagonal. Mark the second set of tucks using the same measurements. Work diagonally from the centre outwards. Sew the second set of tucks across the first.

- Add buttons and beads to the junctions as an alternative decoration to some stitching.

- Try the effect with striped material.

- Explore the technique with wider spacing and larger tucks. Alternatively, mix large and small tucks or, for those with very nimble fingers, create a miniature version.

- Make a panel for a garment perhaps in silk and add beads/pearls/embroidery and *voilà*…a yoke or insert in a bodice.

Experimental play

- Why not make the tucks with a decorative stitch using a contrasting thread? Select the widest stitch design (0.75 cm [¼in] if available). Choose the pattern carefully, as some designs do not reproduce accurately on the uneven surface that is caused

Stage 8 (page 26):
Twisting and stitching each tuck over on the outside edge.

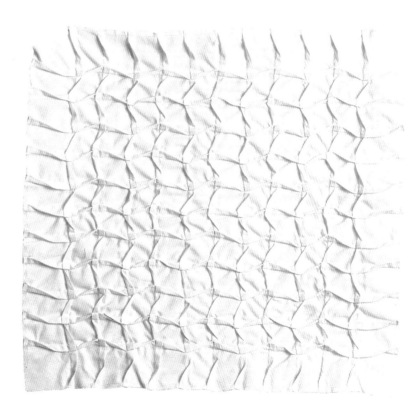

Pin Tucks

A twin needle, two spools of thread and a special presser foot are required for making pin tucks. It is rare for this particular foot to be standard issue in the machine attachments box.

Make sure that you buy the correct sized twin needle when purchasing a pin-tuck foot. There are several different types of pin-tuck feet available: the number of grooves determines the size and spacing of the tucks. The twin needle should fit between the grooves on the underside of the foot.

Setting up your machine

- Attach the foot to the machine and insert the twin needle. Check that the neck of the needle is positioned correctly and the holding screw is firm.

- Thread machine using both spools. On the top of the machine there may be two thread spindles; use one for each thread. If you are lacking a second spindle, put both spools in tandem on the single spindle. Alternatively, another spindle can be created by sticking a knitting needle or similar thin rod beside/near the first spindle (masking tape is ideal for this).

- Some machines have a metal disc in the centre of the tension dial, and these models should be threaded by placing one thread either side of the metal disc. Others are threaded by placing both threads through the same channel. Try not to twist the threads before threading the needles. The thread spools should weigh much the same to prevent the top tension becoming unbalanced.

- Finally, tighten up the top thread tension, i.e. turn to a higher number or towards the (+) sign. Tighter thread tension usually creates a more pronounced pin tuck.

Creating Pin Tucks

1. Start stitching with the presser foot sitting on the fabric, and sew quite slowly and carefully, as twin needles are fragile. Sewing on the diagonal/bias of the fabric in preference to stitching down the straight grain seems to emphasize the raised appearance of the pin tucks.

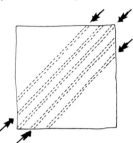

2. Alternate the stitching direction to prevent the material distorting. Aligning one of the grooves in the foot with a previously stitched tuck keeps the lines straight. Check that the groove remains on the same tuck – no deviations allowed!

3. Now, sit comfortably and get thoroughly bored, trundling up and down the fabric in straight lines!

Experimenting with Pin Tucks

- Place a cord underneath the material for a more prominent tuck. (Some machines have a small hole in the sole plate through which the cord can be fed so it runs through automatically as you sew.) Hold the end of the cord as you start and ensure that it remains in the centre of the foot and does not slip out. The grooves of the foot feed it through. (Being of a lazy nature, I have to admit that I never use cord!)

- Use two different-coloured threads in the machine to add variety to the stitch appearance.

- For intriguing and fascinating patterns, sew a grid of straight or randomly curved tucks in different directions.

- Produce a large piece of pin-tucked fabric, then cut it up and use for patchwork (see photograph on page 16). Sacrilege, but effective!

CROSSED-OVER TUCKS

This is an elegant yet elementary technique that is easy to sew. There are many opportunities for textural embellishment, adornment and creative exploration – a real 'must do' for all those twitchers and tweakers out there!

The basic technique consists of two wide tucks; one tuck lies in one direction and the other crosses over it (hence the name). After stitching, each tuck is pressed flat and evenly over the seam. A 'knot' is formed at the intersection of the crossed tucks.

Manipulate the completed design in a wide variety of interesting ways:

- Tuck extra pieces of fabric under the folds.

- Embellish the space between the tucks or cover the area in a different material.

- Twiddle the 'knotty' sections in a variety of ways.

- Add machine or hand embroidery, beads and buttons.

To add more ornamentation and enhance this attractive geometrical pattern. The potential for creative play is huge.

Calico Creation
75 × 75cm (30 × 30in)
Four Crossed-Over Tuck Blocks sewn together. Free-motion machine quilted on polyester wadding.
Jennie Rayment

One Crossed-Over Tuck Square

Finished size: 14cm (5½in) approximately

1. Cut one 20cm (8in) square.

2. Fold the square diagonally with the R/S out.

3. Parallel to this fold, sew a 2.5cm (1in) or more seam. This creates a wide tuck.

4. Open the squares and flatten the tuck by pushing a thin rod/ruler/bar or even a knitting needle inside it. Press the tuck evenly and equally over the seam.

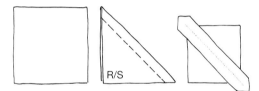

Tip: *Bias bars are remarkably good for this process. These are different sized strips of plastic or metal often used to create bias strips for 'Celtic' type and Stained Glass designs. Both types are heatproof and can be ironed over. They are available in many quilting and craft shops.*

5. Fold the square diagonally again across the other corners.

6. Repeat the measurement and sew the same-sized tuck. Pin either side of the first tuck before sewing the second to prevent the edges catching or twisting over in the next line of stitching. Open and press as before.

7. Baste the outer edge of the tucks, keeping the stitching close to the raw edge.

Textural enhancement

*   Technically, the design is now finished and could be left, though the tucks may shift unless stitched in place. In addition the block is a trifle boring, with just flat tucks and a 'knot' in the centre. Why not sew a decorative machine stitch down the centre of the tucks to hold the layers and add a touch of embellishment?

*   Secure the four corners of the 'knot' with a small hand or machine stitch or attach a decorative stitch, bead or button to the centre. Roll the sides of the tucks inwards, secure flat or bring the sides together and hold in place with an upright bar-tack.

*   For more creative impact, fold the edges of the knot together and/or roll the tucks.

*   Scrunch the 'knot' into a bow. Gather up the 'knot' with three or more small hand running stitches. After gathering, pass the needle through all the layers and secure the 'knot' firmly on the back. A bead or small button could be attached at the same time.

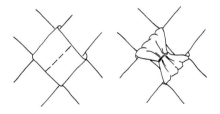

*   Add another textural dimension by inserting four Sharon Squares (page 51) under the centre 'knot'. Stitch the corners of the 'knot' and along the edges of the tucks to hold in place. Roll the central fold of each Sharon Square to make a petal shape.

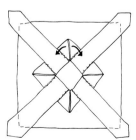

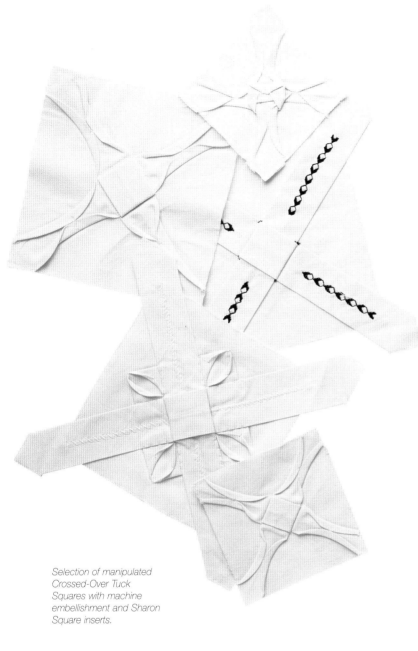

Selection of manipulated Crossed-Over Tuck Squares with machine embellishment and Sharon Square inserts.

Twice Crossed-Over Tuck Block.

• Cut four small squares in the same or a contrasting-coloured material. Fold these squares into triangles and insert at the centre under the tucks. Stitch along the sides of the tucks to hold the triangles in place. Roll back the folded edge of each inserted triangle to form a neat arc and tuck a Somerset Patch (page 50) underneath. Stitch these in place, sewing through all the layers.

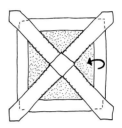 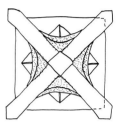

Twice Crossed-Over Tuck

Double up the design for a really interesting concept.

1. Cut a 30cm (12in) or larger square.

2. Fold diagonally (R/S out), pin, and sew two lines of stitch: first line 1.25cm (½in) from folded edge, second line 4cm (1½in) from the first. Flatten and press both sections (one narrow tuck lies on top of a wider one).

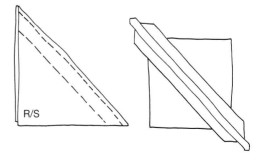

3. Repeat the same technique on the other diagonal by folding the square the other way. Press flat. Baste round the edges and play!

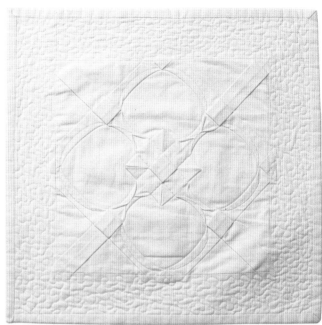

Crossed-Over Tucks block

Finished size: 30 × 30cm (12 × 12in) approximately

1. Cut one 50cm (19in) square.

2. Mark the midpoints of all the sides *on the R/S. Fold in half diagonally – R/S on the outside.*

3. Rule a line 2.5cm (1in) away from and parallel to the diagonal fold. Sew along the drawn line.

4. On one side of this diagonal tuck, fold the fabric on the marked midpoints (fold exactly at the point where the mark touches edge of fabric), and rule a line 2.5cm (1in) from the fold. Pin, and stitch on the line.

5. Repeat on the other side, folding exactly on the marked midpoints. Three large tucks are formed running diagonally across the fabric.

6. Press all three tucks open and flat, ensuring that each tuck is lying evenly either side of the seam. Turn over and press the W/S lightly to remove any creases.

7. Fold on the other diagonal. Pin either side of the three tucks to prevent the tucks catching in the next seam. Rule a line 2.5cm (1in) from the fold and sew. Fold exactly on the midpoint marks (do not unfold the previously pressed tucks). Press the tucks open and flat. Magically, the fabric has returned to a square with a lattice of tucks.

Crossed-Over Tucks Blocks
38 × 38cm (15 × 15in)
Sharon Square inserts.

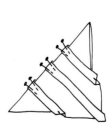

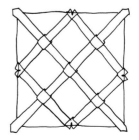

8. Before beginning any manipulation, it is advisable to place a lightweight stabilizer under the fabric such as a thin batting/wadding, or a fine interfacing. (Omitting the stabilizer may result in the distortion of the tucked sample.) Pin the tucked sample to the stabilizer.

Ideas for manipulating this block

- Scrunch up, roll or secure the 'knots', as discussed in the first part of this chapter.

- Roll the tucks together and anchor with a vertical bar-tack, or stitch flat (see photograph opposite).

- Twist one side of the tucks only, producing a curved appearance. Hold the edge of the tuck down with hand stitching or use the Blind Hem stitch (page 11).

- Insert a contrasting-coloured piece of fabric in the space between the tucks. Place this underneath the larger tucks and secure by stitching along the original set of tucks. Fill some or all of the spaces (see photograph on

page 35). Why not select a pictorial design? Think carefully before you cut – the pieces need to be cut on the diagonal (see photograph on page 111).

- Make a tiny 'Crossed-Over Tucks' panel from a 12cm (5in) square with a 1cm (½in) flattened tuck. Insert in the space.

- Fold a square diagonally, insert under the tucks. Stitch in place, and roll back the folded edge. For extra embellishment, tuck some form of folded squares underneath (pages 50–53).

- Embellish the spaces between the tucks with a decorative pattern or a little quilting (see photograph on page 29).

Crossed-Over Tuck Block
30 × 30 cm (12 × 12in) Mounted on polyester batting with coloured inserts and Somerset Patches.

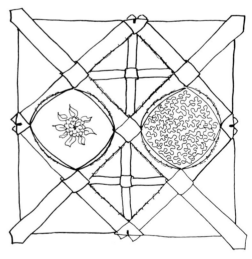

Adding a border
Once all the twiddling and fiddling, nipping and tucking is finished, add the border.

1. Align the border with the raw edge or move it inwards to cover the half 'knots'.

2. Position the seams exactly where required using the technique described on page 12.

3. After the border has been attached, trim the edges and any excess stabilizer.

Design development for Crossed-Over Tucks blocks

- Make a centre panel and add further borders with more textured designs.

- Four blocks can be joined to make a larger panel, but it is easier to cut a bigger piece of material than attempt to match the tucks on four separate pieces. Mark the larger piece at even intervals along all sides. Fold on a set of diagonal marks etc.

- Change the lattice network from squares to rectangles by marking the sides at unequal intervals. Make the tucks as described previously. Trim square afterwards.

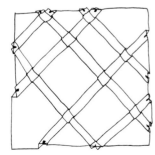

- Instead of making the tucks on the diagonal (bias), make the tucks straight across (from side to side). Be very adventurous and make these

tucks at Fibonacci-related spacing, i.e. 1, 1, 2, 3, 5, 8, etc. Mark the width of the tucks when drafting initially. In the diagram, the tucks were 1in wide with 1in, 1in, 2in, 3in, etc. gaps between. The unit of measurement can be any size, providing the relationship is 1, 1, 2, 3, etc.

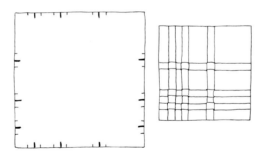

- How about alternating the sizes, with large and small tucks mixed evenly or randomly? Explore the effect of an abstract arrangement for an intriguing textural dimension.

- Experiment with the Crossed-Over Tucks technique in different shapes, such as an equilateral (60°) triangle.

- Explore the effect of Crossed-Over Tucks at different angles in all sorts of shapes – any angle can be selected although the finished panel may need trimming afterwards.

Crossed-Over Tucks Panel
46 × 46cm (18 × 18in) Trumpets with Baltimore Rosebuds on corners. Origami Twist panels. Free-motion machine quilted. Jennie Rayment

Crossed-Over Tucks border

This creative panel makes an innovative frame for quilts and wall hangings or a decorative band in a garment. Colour can be added with folded inserts and/or laid under the tucks. The mathematics are fairly simple: when complete the panel measures approximately two-thirds of the original strip. In doubt, do a test sample.

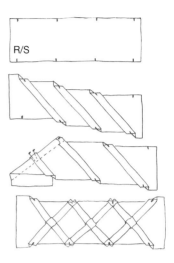

1   Cut a strip of any width and mark out in squares, e.g. a 13cm (5in) strip is marked out at 13cm (5in) intervals. Leave a gap approximately 5cm (2in) either end to allow for any mathematical errors.

2. Make the first set of diagonal tucks. Press flat. Do not panic about the curious appearance of the strip; the second set of tucks will straighten it. Make the second set of tucks and press flat.

3. Baste the edges to hold the tucks in place before attaching to the quilt. Manipulate the tucks, twiddle the central 'knot' and insert colour or folded squares as previously described.

Calico with Colour
70 × 70cm (27½ × 27½in) Crossed-Over Tucks block and border with hand-dyed coloured inserts. Free-motion machine quilting. Jennie Rayment

Calico Circles
53 × 66cm (21 × 26in)
Top right: thirty-six 0.75cm
(¼in) tucks with bias
binding. Lower left: twenty
2cm (¾in) opened and
flattened tucks, 'Babies in
Baskets' inserted under
binding. Free-motion
machine quilted and applied
to calico background on
polyester wadding.
Jennie Rayment

TUCKED CIRCLES

Standing at the kitchen sink peeling the mouldy skin off an elderly mushroom, my attention was attracted by the ridged lines of gills radiating from the stalk. Surely one could create this effect in material? A tuck would resemble one of the gills so why not tuck up a circle?

A strip of straight tucks is marked initially at equal centimetres/inches intervals, but tucked circles have to be drafted in even divisions of 360°. I marked my first successful circle at 9° intervals and made forty tucks (360 divided by 9 = 40) but 10° divisions are much easier to read on the protractor. As a bonus, only 36 tucks have to be made – a great saving in effort!

It is possible to use any equal division of 360°, such as 12°, 15°, 18° or 20°, etc. A tuck is formed on every mark: therefore, if you select 12° divisions (360 divided by 12 = 30) only 30 tucks have to be made to complete the circle.

In addition, a tucked circle has to have a hole in the centre; until I appreciated this, my first attempt was a puckered mess. I rapidly discovered that the seam width and quantity of tucks determined the size of the central hole. The centre hole is drawn with a pair of compasses (known more commonly these days as a compass) set at the correct distance; then it is cut out before any tucks are made.

The big problem is calculating the size of hole to cut, and this does involve hard sums! The measurement of the circumference has to allow for the quantity and size of the tucks, plus a certain amount of additional space so that the tucks can lie flat when pressed. It is easier sometimes to guess the size of the central hole and if it proves too small, cut the hole bigger.

Size of centre circle for 0.75cm (¼in) tucks

Measurements are rounded up for ease of circle construction. Set the compass at the given radius measurement.

36 tucks: 10° = 13cm (4½in) radius
30 tucks: 12° = 11cm (3¾in) radius
24 tucks: 15° = 8.75cm (2⅝in) radius
20 tucks: 18° = 7.25cm (2⅛in) radius
18 tucks: 20° = 6.5cm (2¼in) radius

Don't fuss too much. Do not forget… **You can't go wrong – it is just a little different**.

Creating a Tucked Circle

1. Rip out a large square of fabric. Fold in half and half again forming a smaller square. Fold this square diagonally from the corners at **A** to the centre at **B**. For greater accuracy, fold one half to the front and the other to the back. Press gently.

 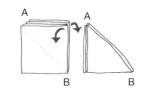

2. Check that the square is folded correctly – all four corners at **A** should be opposite the centre **B**. Failure to fold correctly may result in four quarter circles, not a whole one. Disaster!

3. Measure the distance from **C** to **B**. Make several marks across the fabric at this distance to form an arc across the material. Measure each time from **B**.

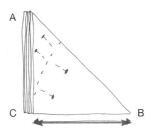

4. Pin the layers together both sides of the marks; cut carefully along the arc. Open out. (This technique is ideal for cutting circular tablecloths or other large circles.)

5. Draw a cross in the centre of the circle. Insert the point of the compass in the centre of the cross and draw the relevant-sized inner circle. Use a protractor to measure the selected degree interval, e.g. every 10°. (Check the midpoint of the protractor is aligned with the drawn cross.) Reverse the protractor to mark the lower half.

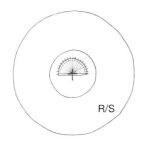

6. Line up the ruler with the centre cross and one of the degree points; mark *outside the inner circle* and the *inside of the outer circle*. *Accuracy is important.* The marks on both the inner and outer circle should be spaced equally, albeit at different distances. Tape the circle to a flat surface to keep it smooth while you work.

7. Identify several sets of corresponding marks with a small X.

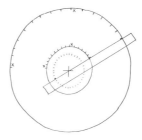

8. Cut out the inner circle. Fold the fabric exactly on a corresponding set of marks and sew a 0.75cm (¼in) seam. Repeat on each set of marks. Alternate the direction of the stitching to prevent distortion and use a thread saver (page 10).

Tip: *A tuck is formed by a line of stitching **parallel** to the fold, **not a diagonal** one as in a dart. Watch the seam allowance. Do not drift in or out at the end of the seams. Take care to align the correct sets of corresponding marks.*

9. Check the crosses line up – if you start a tuck with an X one end and not the other, stop! Unpick the tucks until a correct set of corresponding marks is reached.

10. Press all the tucks in the same direction on completion. Press both sides of the material well. The circle should lie flat. Sometimes the finished result refuses to lie flat and resembles a lampshade. There is a sneaky way to overcome this problem (see Tip).

Tip: *By hand (use a thick or doubled thread), sew around the central hole; draw up until the circle lies flat. Any excess bunching of the tucks will be concealed when the centre is applied. Have faith!*

11. Lay a spare piece of material under the centre hole and pin in place. Baste round the inner circle edge, securing the tucks to the spare piece. Do not worry if the hole is not circular, the next stage will improve the appearance.

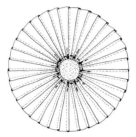

Applying the centre

12. Measure across the centre between the lines of basting to find the diameter of the central section. Set a compass for half this measurement (the radius). Draw a circle on some paper; cut out. This paper circle will be the template for the centre section.

Tip: *Why not experiment with variously sized paper circles and decide which size looks best visually? Providing the paper circle covers the basting, it can be made any size.*

13. Cut a rough circle of fabric approximately 1.25cm (½in) larger than the paper. Pin the paper to the W/S of the fabric circle.

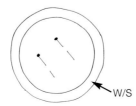

14. Baste the fabric to the paper; feed the pleats in with a wooden skewer (page 13).

15. Pin to the centre of the tucked circle and stitch in place – the Blind Hem stitch is a good choice (page 11). Leave the paper inside the fabric for the moment.

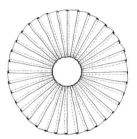

Create texture – twist the Tucks
(At this stage, the tucked circle could be mounted on wadding/batting. Pin the layers well.)

16. Stitch round in a series of concentric circles, working from the centre out. *The distance between each circular line of stitch is your choice. Do all the distances have to be equal?* Twist a few tucks by hand to view the finished effect before stitching.

17. Measure the first line of stitching from the newly applied circle and mark the material in a series of light pencil dots. Stitch on this line twisting the tucks over as you sew (the dots are concealed as the tucks are twisted). Continue marking, measuring from the centre each time.

18. Twist the tucks over in opposite directions as each circular line is sewn. (This is the same technique as twisting straight tucks (see page 17). This method, although very accurate, is fairly time-consuming.

Is there another way?

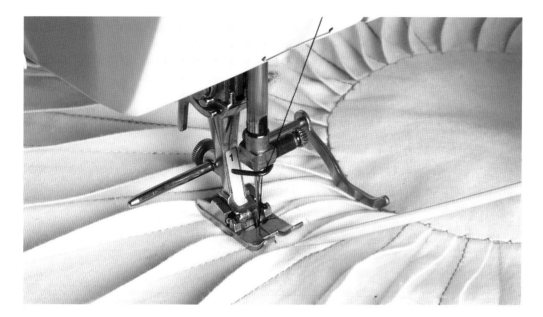

Achieve the same effect with the quilting guide (page 18).

1. Set the desired measurement between the edge of the guide and the machine needle. Sew the first circle – the edge of the quilting guide is aligned with the rim of the applied centre.

2. Sew the second circle and this time measure the selected distance from the first circle of stitch. Continue in this manner. Stop stitching approximately 0.75cm (¼in) from the outside edge of the circle.

TIP: *As most quilting guides fit on the right-hand side of the presser foot, the work has to be stitched anticlockwise. Accuracy is important because the edge of the guide traces the previously stitched circle line as shown in the photograph. Do not wobble as this will be repeated in the next line of stitching!*

• Do the tucks have to be twisted on every line of stitch? Leave a section of the tucks flat then embellish this area afterwards (see the photograph of the Tucked Calico Circle).

Completing the Tucked Circle

1. Unpick the basting from the applied centre.

2. Turn the work over and slit the spare piece of fabric on the back; remove the paper through the gap. Alternatively, trim the layers to 0.75cm (¼in) from the stitching line of the applied centre, then remove the paper.

For a small circular quilt or hanging

Mount the circle on batting/wadding and a backing fabric. Pin, tack-gun or baste the layers together before quilting the layers. (Sewing round the outer edge of the applied centre and restitching over or beside one or more of the other sewn lines is probably sufficient.) Bind the outside edge with a bias strip.

Tucked Calico Circle
68 × 68cm (27 × 27in)
Featuring a flat area of tucks, satin-stitched centre and bias-bound edge. Tucked Circle applied to a square then free-motion machine quilted.
Jennie Rayment

Box indicates
detail discussed

*Detail from **OTT** (page 121). Bound edge with Somerset Patches inserted. Ruched centre.*

To increase the size or make it square

Cut another piece of fabric the desired size or shape. Lay the tucked circle on top and pin in place carefully. Baste the outer edge of the circle to the other piece of fabric before binding with a bias strip. Stitch the binding in place by hand or machine (see Blind Hem stitch, page 11).

Embellishing the Tucked Circle

- Embroider over the stitching or round the edge with a decorative pattern.

- Apply an ornamental ribbon or braid to the centre or across the stitching.

- For a really fancy finish, insert Somerset Patches, Prairie Points, 'Babies in Baskets' (pages 50–53), a small frill or some gathered lace under the binding before stitching in place. Sew the edge of the binding over the inserted decoration.

- Apply a circle of ruched material, appliqué some three-dimensional fabric flowers or another textural design to the centre for a creative finish.

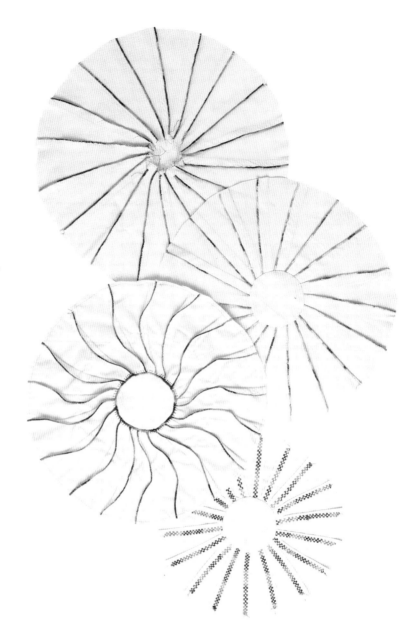

Experiment with Tucked Circles

Instead of making complete circles of stitch, explore the appearance of a stitched spiral radiating out from the centre; twist the tucks as the spiral expands. This requires a little bit of artistic licence as it does not quite 'work' totally evenly. Try it and see!

Embellish the Tucks

Satin-stitch down the edge of the tucks with one of the many fabulous threads that are available these days. Choose from gleaming metallic to fabulously variegated ones. The finished effect is fantastic, despite taking ages to complete.

- Make the tucks and, before twisting, satin-stitch down the edge. Fill the top and bottom bobbin with the same colour or experiment with two contrasting ones. Set a narrow close zigzag. Sew down the edge, 'zigging' in and 'zagging' off, covering the edge of the tuck.

Tip: *Metallic threads have a nasty habit of shredding or unravelling as you sew. Specialist needles are available, although a size or two larger machine needle (14/90 or 16/100) than the usual (10/70 or 12/80) may prove equally as good. The bigger eye on these needles allows the thread to run through more easily. This may resolve the problem.*

- Alternatively, apply a thread to the edge of the tuck (page 21). The selection of decorative threads and edgings is so diverse, it is difficult to choose.

- And then…go one stage further and decorate the tuck with a fancy pattern before manipulating. This is almost like stuffing mushrooms but if time permits – why not?

Vary the number and size of Tucks

The tucks can be spaced on any degree division of a circle, as long as the number divides evenly into 360°. In addition, the width of the tucks can be increased or decreased.

- How about marking the circle at 20° intervals and making larger tucks?

1. Draw an inner circle of 15cm (6in) radius.

2. Sew a 2cm (¾in) seam on each set of marks. These tucks will overlap at the centre.

3. Follow the previous instructions for completion. Do not twist the tucks too many times or the circle will distort.

Tucked Circles marked at 20° (18 tucks) with embellished edgings and different sized tucks. The lowest circle has opened and flattened tucks.

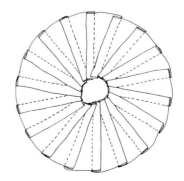

- Changing the number or the width of the tucks may require an alteration to the radius of the inner circle, and calculating the size of the central hole required can be complicated. Solve the problem by making a rough estimate; if too small and it is difficult to make the tucks the desired size, cut the hole larger; if the hole is too large, then adjust the size of the appliquéd centre. (For example, a sunflower has an enormous centre and could be an excellent design inspiration. Who is to say that this wasn't your original intention?)

- Finally, for a most unusual result, change the sizes of the tucks – alternate a wide one with a narrow one. Be consistent; otherwise the circle will not lie flat.

Off-Centre Circle
56 × 56cm (22 × 22in)
Applied to a square. Bound bias edge. Machine quilted with the walking foot.
Jennie Rayment

Move the centre circle

Why not draft a Tucked Circle with the inner circle drawn off-centre? Follow the same construction technique as before then just play!

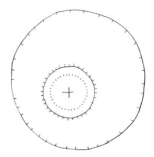

Change the overall shape

Cut a square or another geometric shape and follow the same drafting technique and construction method. The outer edges will need trimming.

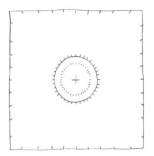

Try drawing the inner circle off-centre!

Open and flatten the tucks

1. Make 1.25cm (½in) or wider tucks. Open and press them flat over the seam (as in Crossed-Over Tucks). The tucks will overlap at the centre.

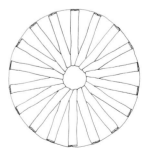

2. Once the centre has been applied, manipulate the edges of the tucks (see Magnolia Dusk, page 120). Why not embellish the tucks with decorative stitch (see the photograph on page 42)?

Take two circles

The finished effect is similar to the spokes of a wheel or a Mariner's Compass (traditional patchwork design).

1. Cut two 40cm (16in) or larger circles. Fold one circle in four to find the centre. Mark the centre on the R/S. Lay the marked circle on top of the other and match the grain lines. Pin both circles together (W/S facing).

2. Draw a 5cm (2in) radius circle in the centre. Divide the circle into twelve (30°) or sixteen (22½°) sections using a protractor. Rule lines across the fabric from side to side. Pin the middle of every section.

3. Cut out the drawn inner circle (cut out both layers simultaneously). Cut on all the lines, forming twelve/sixteen sets of wedges. Number the wedges (small sticky labels are ideal). To avoid confusion, label the top circle 1:12/16 and the bottom circle 1a:12a/16a. **Put the labels on the R/S of the material**. Remove pins and separate all the pieces.

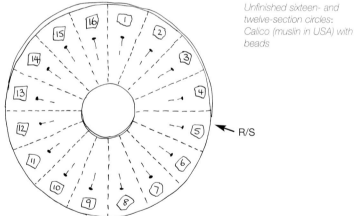

← R/S

Unfinished sixteen- and twelve-section circles: Calico (muslin in USA) with beads

4. Fold all the bottom circle wedges (1a–12a/16a) in half lengthways (R/S out); keep them in the correct order.

Consistency pays!

5. Sew the top circle wedges together, inserting a folded bottom wedge into the seam *but* turn the bottom wedge round so the wider edge is to the centre. Look at the diagram carefully. Use a 0.75cm (¼in) S/A.

Twelve-Section Circle
53 × 53cm (21 × 21in)
Completed circle applied to
a square. Bound edge
embellished with decorative
stitching. Free-motion
machine quilting.
Jennie Rayment

6. Sew the wedges together in pairs, i.e. 1 and 2, then 3 and 4 etc. Stitch the pairs together into fours, then into eights, and then sew together to form the circle. Sew all the sections from the centre outwards.

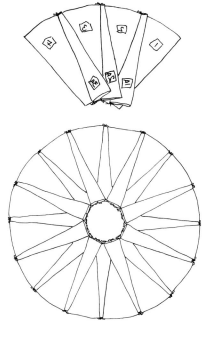

7. Remove the labels before pressing all the inserted sections open and flat. Overlap every other one. Cover the centre with an applied circle (page 39). Embellish and twiddle the inserted sections as desired.

Develop the design

- Two contrasting-coloured materials work most effectively with this design. For an even more colourful effect, cut out several circles and interchange the pieces. Careful labelling will avoid confusion.

- Change the size of the drawn centre circle and see what happens.

- Do not turn the inserted (1a–12a/16a) pieces round but keep the wider edge on the outside. The finished effect is reminiscent of wheel-spokes or rays.

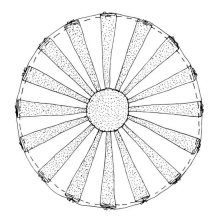

- Try the same technique with two ovals, squares, triangles, rectangles and other geometric forms. The completed shape may need a certain amount of trimming.

*Detail from **Cosmic Happening** (page 124). Off-centre circle inserted in a square.*

Experimental play

- What would happen if the centre circle were drawn off-centre? Try it! (Not my idea but suggested by an interested engineer chap.) The circle in the diagram below is divided into twelve 30° sections.

centre. Follow the same drafting instructions and construction method. Trim the edges on completion.

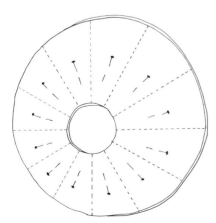

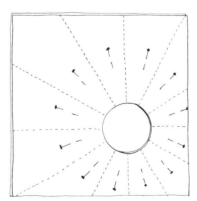

- Now take two squares and try this latest suggestion with the centre square drawn off-

- Finally…take two different-sized circles or other geometric shapes. Insert the smaller one into the larger. The inserted section has to be arranged carefully (at a slight angle) so that the seam covers the raw end.

FOLDED SQUARES

There are many ways to fold a square and this chapter contains just a few of them. The simplest way to fold a square is in half, either straight across to make a rectangle or on the diagonal to form a triangle. The triangle has greater potential for creative design, mainly because the fold is on the bias.

*Detail from **Amish Friendship Stars** (page 49)*

Take two squares

This design creates an interesting textured corner for a border or sashing.

1. Cut two equal-sized squares. Fold one diagonally in half (R/S out) forming a triangle and place on the other square (background) R/S up. Align all the raw edges and pin before basting the layers together.

2. Once basted, roll back the folded bias edge of the triangle in an arc. Secure the fold with a few stitches, or sew the entire edge with the Blind Hem stitch (page 11) or any other decorative pattern of your choice.

Create a double arc

Stitch the centre of the bias fold to the backing square. Roll back either side of the centre point. For a really scalloped edge, catch the bias fold in several places before rolling.

Add ornamentation

Tuck a Somerset Patch (page 50) under the rolled fold. Stitch in place. Why stop at one Patch – how about three? Pad the pocket under the triangle for more three-dimensional impact.

Innovative patchwork

Replace any square patch composed of two equal triangles (often called a divided or half-divided square) with two squares (see page 47).

Half-divided square

Just think of the difference that could be made to a whole range of patchwork designs! The basic Amish Friendship Star, an ordinary Eight-Pointed Star or many other similar patterns would look radically different if the relevant parts of the design were replaced with this technique. Once the folded edges are rolled, curves would replace straight lines. As a bonus, there are no triangular templates needed, just cut squares of fabric.

Trim

Trim part of the underside of the folded square before basting it to the background one. This will reduce the bulk in the seams.

Take this idea further

1. Stitch two triangles of different coloured materials together to make a square. Trim the seam well. Press open and flat.

2. Fold the square diagonally in half on the seam. Place on the background square. Pin and baste the outer edges. Roll back the seamed edge to reveal the other colour.

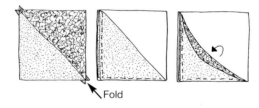

Fold

Create more texture

(This is only suitable for fabrics with no obvious R/S.)

1. Tuck one corner under before placing on the background square. Pin and baste raw edges then roll back both folded edges.

2. Insert a Somerset Patch (see next section) under both folded edges for more embellishment.

Eight-Point Star
43 × 43cm (17 × 17in)
Folded squares with
Baltimore Rosebuds and
Somerset Patches.
Jennie Rayment

Amish Friendship Stars
158 × 158cm (62 × 62in)
Folded squares with Inserted
Rectangle border. Free-
motion machine quilting.
Jennie Rayment

Textured edgings and inserts

All the following techniques can be made from any square. Cut one to begin; trim the edges if too large or cut a bigger one if too small. (Really technical stuff!) Circles can also be folded in all of the following ways but squares are simpler to cut.

Somerset Patch

In Britain, this way of folding a square is often called a Somerset Patch, or, less frequently, Mitred or Folded Patchwork. The USA and other parts of the world refer to the design as Shark's Tooth.

It is ideal for any straight or gently arced edge/seam.

1. Fold a square in half, making a rectangle.

2. Fold **A** and **B** over to touch raw edges, making a right-angled (90°) triangle. Baste the raw edges.

To add more textural intrigue – before basting the raw edge

1. Fold the top flaps inwards and under; conversely, fold the flaps outwards. Baste the raw edge. (Thinner materials are preferable as this additional fold adds bulk.)

2. Add another colour by making the initial square from two equal rectangles. Trim the seam before folding as described above. One colour will be on the outside and the second one revealed in the centre once the folds are opened.

3. Adjust the shape subtly by bringing the two folded flaps to meet at the centre. Baste and trim the base level before inserting.

Alter the angle completely
(This was a neat idea shown by a student. She deserves top marks for lateral thinking.)

1. Fold a square into a rectangle then fold each side in half.

2. Take **A** to **C,** then **B** to **D**. Fold the flap of the top section outwards as much as you like. Repeat with the flap underneath. Trim the shape before insertion. (The triangle formed is approximately 60°.)

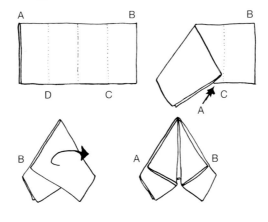

- Six of these fit together to make an intriguing hexagonal design (see photograph on page 51). Lay the shapes on a fabric base. Match the points at the centre and sew to the base material. Roll the folds and secure in relevant places with a few stitches. Baste round the outer edges and trim off the excess material. Add a border if required. Although the finished design is thickly layered, it makes an interesting block with lots of twiddleable possibilities. Have a play!

Six 60° Somerset Patches
35 × 35cm (14 × 14in)
Sewn onto a base, and before trimming along the drawn line.

Baltimore Rosebud

A nifty notion for tucking into a pocket or under folds for additional ornamentation. It can be made from a square but a rectangle is less bulky.

Fold the one long side of the rectangle over to hide the raw edge. Fold into a Somerset Patch (see page 50). Refold both corners inwards to overlap at the centre. Baste.

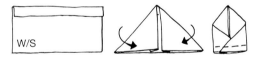

Tip: *A good-quality ribbon can be substituted for the rectangle of fabric (no need to fold the edge over). A strip of material with one raw edge overlocked/serged could also be used – the stitched edge would add a decorative touch.*

Sharon Square

(This pattern was named after an American lass who asked the name of the technique. There was no specific title for this idea so we decided to use her name.)

Use this design when a right-angled insertion is required, e.g. a corner.

1. Fold a square into a triangle first. Bring **A** and **B** to touch **C**.

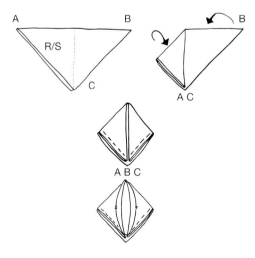

2. Once inserted in the selected place, roll the central folds outward to create a petal shape.

Developing the design

- Increase the colour potential by making the original square from two triangles. Stitch the triangles together. Trim and clip seam before folding. One colour will be on the outside, the second colour is revealed when the central folds of the Sharon Square are rolled back.

Prairie Points

These can be made singularly (Trumpets, page 64) and inserted into a pocket or under a fold. Several individual Prairie Points can be slotted inside each other for a decorative edge. A selection of different sizes would vary the appearance of the edging.

Prairie Points should be used on a straight or gently arced edge or seam.

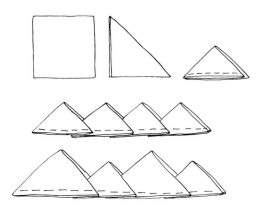

A *continuous row of Prairie Points* can be constructed from a single strip of material. (This is an old technique and not my own idea.) The finished band is thickly layered with a level edge. The length of the strip can vary, but the width is twice the size of the Prairie Points. Remember to add the S/A before calculating the desired finished width of the fabric.

Continuous band of Prairie Points

To make a 95 × 4.5cm (38 × 1⅛in) band of continuous Prairie Points:

1. Cut one strip 95 × 20cm (38 × 8in), i.e. twice the measurement of the Prairie Points plus the S/As. Fold in half lengthways.

2. Commence 5cm (2in) from one end. Make nine 10cm (4in) cuts at 10cm (4in) intervals

along one long edge (dividing into square sections). Repeat on the other edge but *start at the other end*.

3. Trim the rectangles from each end. Fold each 'square' on the diagonal as shown (second diagram below).

4. Work from right to left; fold first (lower) triangle in half; fold up (onto upper row); fold second (upper) triangle over this one. Repeat the pattern with remaining triangles. All the triangles should slot into each other.

5. Baste the raw edge before inserting in a seam.

Try this in a striped fabric!

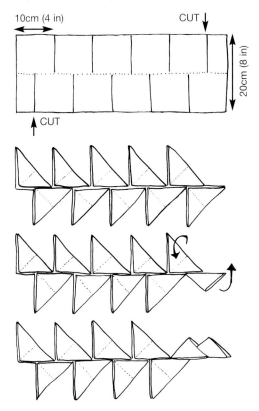

'Baby in a Basket'

This is ideal for a straight or gently arced edge.

1. Press a square diagonally in half (R/S out), open out and fold on the other diagonal and press again. Try not to obliterate the first diagonal crease as you press the second one.

2. Fold in half (R/S out) to form a rectangle. Lift up the top layer of the rectangle and tuck corner **A** inside.

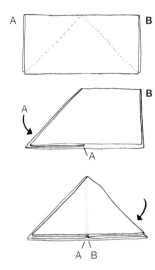

3. Repeat with **B** corner on the other side. A triangle is formed with two folds on either side (**A** and **B** touch inside). Align the raw edges.

4. Bring *one top fold* from *each side* to lie flush in the centre. Baste lower edge and trim.

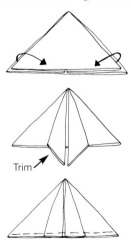

5. This shape can now be inserted in a seam and the centre folds rolled outwards and/or the outer folds rolled inwards.

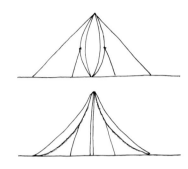

Variation on the Baltimore Rosebud (page 51)

Fold the corners in again overlapping them evenly across the centre of the shape. Baste the layers and trim the excess material from the base. Experiment with rolling the folds.

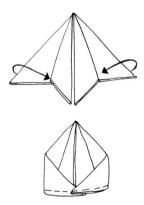

A last thought

Look in books and at articles on origami techniques – if paper can be folded in a set design, so can fabric. In addition, origami created from material has many more exciting manipulative possibilities than paper. It flexes more easily: folds can be twisted, pockets padded and any bias edge rolled. Select a crisp fabric that creases well and consider overlocking/sergeing the raw edges to prevent fraying.

INTERLOCKED SQUARES AND MORE

This simple and effective textured creation is ideal for blocks and borders. All kinds of materials from diaphanous voiles to sumptuous silks can be used. Use of different colours or tints, tones and shades of the same hue will enhance the dynamics of the design (great phrase!).

The basic Interlocked Square block consists of four equal-sized squares; each square is folded diagonally and overlapped in sequence. The last square is tucked under the first. To complete the block, the folded diagonal edge of each section is rolled outwards producing a small square hole at the centre. A smaller square of fabric (approximately one quarter of the initial square) is placed beneath the hole and stitched in place.

One Interlocked Square block

Finished size: 15 × 15cm (6 × 6in)

Seam allowance: 1cm (⅜in)

1. Cut four 17cm (6¾in) squares. Press all the squares diagonally in half with the R/S out.

2. Lay one folded square with the right-angled corner on the left. Insert a pin in the right-hand corner of the triangle.

3   Place a second folded square on top and rotate it through 90° (a quarter turn), turning in a *clockwise* direction. The pin is visible and the folded edge is towards the centre.

4. The third square goes on the second and is rotated through 90° in the same manner (pin is still visible).

5. Finally, the fourth square is placed on the third and rotated once more through 90°. *The pin is concealed.* Now, tuck the left-hand corner of the fourth square under the first square to *reveal the pin!* The folded edges of the squares form a diagonal cross.

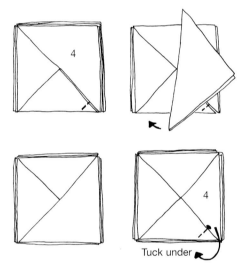

6. Ensure that all the raw edges of the folded squares are aligned. A small gap at the centre does not matter. Pin all the layers carefully with eight pins, two either side of each diagonal fold.

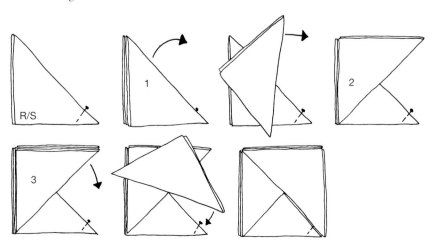

7. Baste closely round the outer edge. Use a small wooden barbecue skewer (page 13), the point of a stitch ripper or bodkin to hold the layers stable and prevent the fold shifting at the corners. The finished design is double-sided. Select one side as the right side.

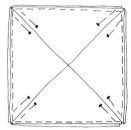

Add a border before manipulating the block

1. Attach the border with a 1cm (⅜in) seam to ensure that all the raw edges of the Interlocked Square are enclosed in the seam.

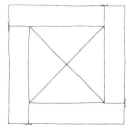

2. After attaching the border, roll out the folded edges as far as possible. Roll each fold equally. (The folded edges of the Interlocked Squares should lie on the border, slightly over the seam.) A *square* hole appears in the centre if the four folded edges have been rolled equally. Turn the block over to check that the rolled edges are lying neatly underneath.

 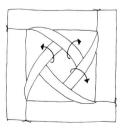

3. Cut a 7.5cm (3in) square of material in any colour and lay under the square hole. Stitch the layers together on the corners or sew round the inner edge of the central hole. This can be done by hand or machine (Blind Hem stitch, page 11). In addition, secure the rolled folds close to the outer edges of the block with a few small stitches.

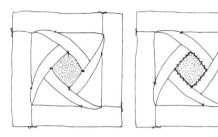

Ideas for developing the Interlocked Square block

• Lay a textured material with an interesting slub or weave under the central space. Cut a small square of some pin-tucked material and use this to fill the centre hole.

• How about a touch of glamour with one of the sparkling metallic or glittering reflective materials that are available these days? Try personalizing the block with a pictorial fabric or a small photograph – special preparations are available to transfer photographs to fabric, or you could glue the picture in place with a fabric resin (do not wash it afterwards).

• Tuck Somerset Patches or Baltimore Rosebuds (pages 50–51) etc. under the rolled edges. Stitch in place.

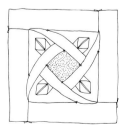

Add more colour

Stitch two contrasting-coloured triangles to form a square.

1. Cut four 17.5cm (6⅞in) squares, two in each colour. Cut diagonally into triangles.

2. Sew two triangles (one of each colour) together (0.75cm [¼in] seam) to make a *square*. Clip the seam and press open.

3. Fold the square on the seam and press again.

4. Make three more squares using the remaining triangles.

5. Create an Interlocked Square with the same coloured side of each square uppermost. The other colour will be revealed as an edging when the folded edges are rolled. Use a further colour to fill the centre.

Mirror-imaging an Interlocked Square block

Rotate the pieces round anticlockwise as shown in the lower diagram.

1. Place the corner of the folded square on the right; put the pin in the left. Remember that

the pieces are now rotated round *anticlockwise*. The pin is a useful guide; rotate the pieces towards the pin.

2. Pin the layers and baste. The completed block is easy to baste as the folds follow the 'flow' of the stitching and do not catch under the presser foot.

3. Check the mirror imaging – lay one anticlockwise (AC) and one clockwise (C) block side by side. *The folds roll back in opposite directions.*

Interlocked Square Block
33 × 33cm (13 × 13in)
Squares made from two coloured triangles. Top-stitching around design.
Jennie Rayment

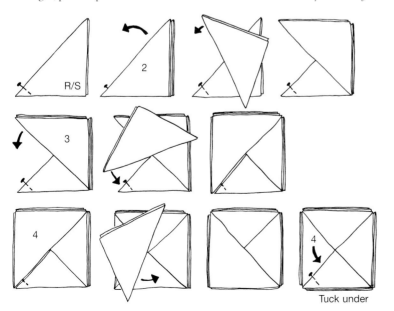

R/S

2

3

4

4

Tuck under

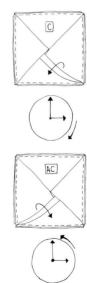

C

AC

Interlocked Square blocks

Combine texture, shape and colour by joining several blocks to make some highly creative, intriguingly different and innovative designs. Use a 1cm (⅜in) seam when joining the blocks (remember to allow for this in any calculations).

Match the folds of each block on the right side, not the raw edges. Getting the folded edges aligned precisely creates a more professional appearance on the R/S; the seams can be juggled somewhat. The 1cm (⅜in) seam should be large enough to include all the raw edges but a certain amount of persuasion may be necessary!

Tip: *As the seams between two or more blocks are very thick, reduce the bulk by trimming each square before interlocking the pieces (fold the corner back prior to cutting and check that the cut section does not show through to the top side).*

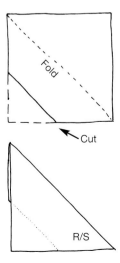

Creative block design

- Join all the blocks before starting to manipulate the folded edges. Roll back the folds once all the sides have been framed with borders or other blocks.

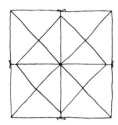

- Join four *clockwise* or four *anticlockwise* units (right-hand photograph above).

- Or sew *two anticlockwise* (AC) and *two clockwise* blocks (C) together and create a very different appearance (left-hand photograph). Label the blocks to avoid confusion – it is all too easy to get in a total muddle when sewing them together!

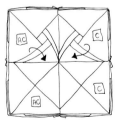

Interlocked Square borders

Join all blocks for the border before manipulating.

- Sew several units rotating in the same direction or pairs of units (clockwise and anticlockwise) as shown on the Textured Sampler quilt (page 6).

- Or insert another layer of differently coloured material in the spaces between pairs of clockwise and anticlockwise units. Tuck the additional fabric under the folds of the Interlocked Square block where possible; alternatively fold the raw edge under before appliquéing in place.

Tip: *Frame any Interlocked Square strip with another border before rolling any folds.*

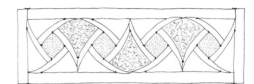

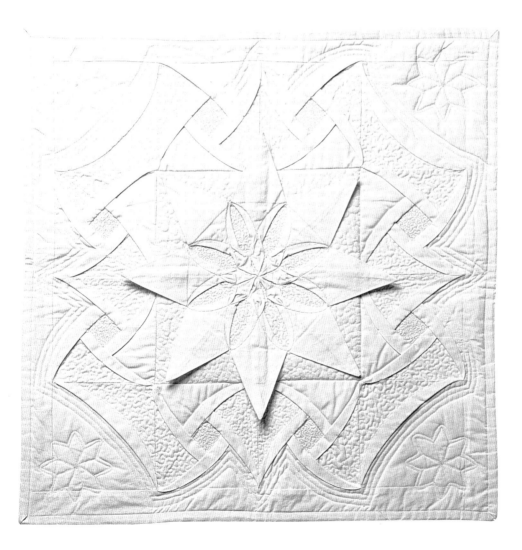

Tarantella
70 × 70cm (27 × 27in)
Eight Inserted Squares Block with Interlocked Square border composed of clockwise and anticlockwise units. All calico (muslin in USA). Free-motion machine quilted.
Jennie Rayment

Four Interlocked Square Blocks
46 × 46cm (18 × 18in)
Corners tucked under. Top-stitched with a twin needle (different threads through each needle).
Jennie Rayment

- Tuck the corner of each square under (do not trim, as described in the Tip on page 57). Construct an Interlocked Square. Roll back both folds of each square. This has a wonderful woven appearance, especially when several units are joined.

How about half the design?

1. Cut three squares the same size, fold two diagonally and lay onto the third.

2. Overlap the folded squares in one corner. Pin and baste in place.

3. Make a mirror image with three more pieces.

Join a number of these blocks for a border, either as a single row or doubled up.

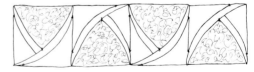

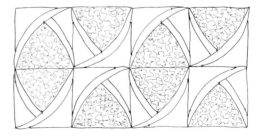

Creative development

- Experiment with colour and/or different materials to add more interest. The effect of stripes and other directional designs are well worth exploring but be careful how the fabric is folded, especially when the units rotate in different directions. Try the designs with coloured transparent materials; as the shapes interweave, the colours will mix.

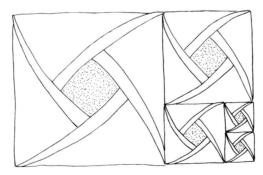

- Make the Interlocking Square blocks in Fibonacci-related sizes (1, 1, 2, 3, 5, 8, etc.). Put them together as a panel.

Interlocked Triangles
69 × 99cm (27 × 39in)
Anticlockwise and
clockwise rotated blocks
(three triangles side up)
joined into hexagons then
applied to background
fabric. Centres embellished
with thread flowers. Free-
motion machine quilting.
Jennie Rayment

- Try interlocking triangles, hexagons and other symmetrical geometric shapes instead of squares.

- Rectangles and other asymmetrical forms can also be interlocked although it may be necessary to mirror-image the fold. Think carefully before folding any irregular shape. Try the idea in paper first – it is cheaper than fabric!

Interlocked Triangles

Each block is composed of three *equilateral* (60°) triangles.

1. Cut out three triangles. Fold each triangle in half across the bias grain and press (R/S out). *The pressed fold has to be across the bias grain* for maximum effectiveness when rolling.

2. Rotate the triangles clockwise, tucking the last one underneath the first. Pin well and baste round the raw edges.

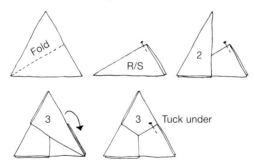

3. Look carefully at both sides: one side has three triangle shapes, the other has three four-sided 'kite' shapes. Choose either side.

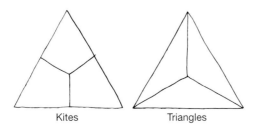

Kites   Triangles

4. Roll back the folded edges of the triangles to create a triangular window. Fill the space with a scrap of the same material, a contrasting colour or a textured fabric. Sew in place.

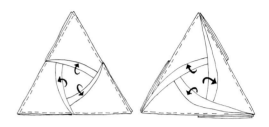

Design ideas

- Combine a mixture of 'kite' or triangle sides and different rotations in a variety of colours to create some amazingly unusual design blocks.

- Make another Interlocked Triangle but rotate the pieces anticlockwise.

- Make six units and rotate three clockwise and three anticlockwise. Join them up to form a hexagon.

- Make six units and alternate the 'kite' and triangle sides. Sew into a hexagon.

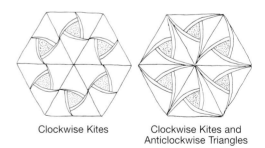

Clockwise Kites   Clockwise Kites and
                         Anticlockwise Triangles

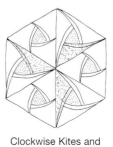

Clockwise Kites and
Triangles

Interlocked Hexagons

Cut several hexagons. Fold in a 'boat' shape on the bias grain. Press.

Three Hexagons

1. Place pin on right-hand side.

2. Lay a folded hexagon on alternate sides. Rotate clockwise.

3. Tuck the third hexagon under the first hexagon to reveal the pin.

4. Pin the layers and baste the raw edges.

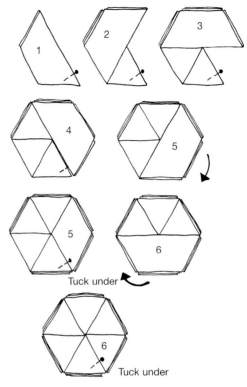

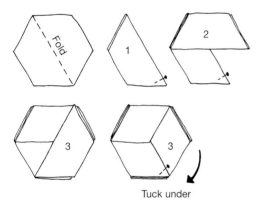

Tuck under

5. Roll back the folded edges, creating a triangular space in the centre.

Six Hexagons

1. Insert a pin on the right-hand side of the first hexagon. (Part of the underside of the hexagons can be trimmed to reduce bulk.)

2. Rotate the remaining five hexagons *clockwise*, laying one on each side. *Both the fifth and the sixth are tucked under the first hexagon* to reveal the pin. Pin and baste raw edges.

3. Roll back the folded edges to reveal a hexagonal hole in the centre.

Four Hexagons

These form a cross when interlocked. Magically, a diamond-shaped space is revealed in the centre when the folded edges are rolled.

Combining

For an amazingly intricate hanging, combine a variety of all types of Interlocked Hexagons. Experiment with rotating clockwise or vice versa. Explore the use of different colours both for the folded hexagons and for filling in the spaces. Try it, and play.

Interlocked Hexagons
50 × 50cm (20 × 20in)
Seven calico and silk
Interlocked Hexagons (six
sets of three and one set of
six hexagons) joined to form
larger hexagon. Machine
applied with satin stitch to a
background silk square. An
additional colour inserted
under the folds of the
centre hexagon. Free-
motion machine quilting.
Jennie Rayment

TRUMPETS

Trumpets are nothing more than squashed and inserted Prairie Points. The design was created while twiddling idly (as one does) with a decorative edging of Prairie Points. To my complete amazement, the Prairie Points could be opened and flattened into all kinds of very different forms.

Daylight dawned and there was an instant generation of great excitement because the possibilities for textural play are amazing. The shape can be stuffed, twitched, tweaked, fiddled and generally manoeuvred into many patterns. A most versatile creation.

Initially, they were called Cornets due to a vague resemblance to an ice-cream cone, although the shape is reminiscent of an old fashioned ear trumpet or the brass horn from a Victorian gramophone. For some reason the name Trumpets proved more popular.

Constructing a Trumpet

1. Fold a square of any size in half diagonally with the R/S out, and then diagonally in half again. This makes a smaller triangle with two folds one end and one fold the other. What could be easier?

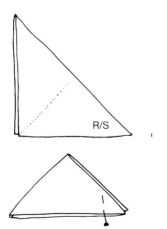

2. Make sure both folded edges lie absolutely flush before pinning the layers. Baste the shape close to the raw edges using the longest machine stitch.

3. Start the basting at the 'two-fold' end (by pin) and sew towards the single fold (other end). Drop the machine needle into the 'two-fold' end *before* lowering the presser foot and commencing basting. (See basting advice on page 9.)

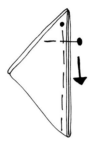

4. The Trumpet is normally inserted into a seam before manipulation. Once inserted or appliquéd the Trumpet can be rolled, folded, twisted, padded and pleated and/or have a textural insert of one form or other in the open end/pocket. The manipulated shape is secured in place with a few small stitches by hand or machine wherever necessary.

Silk Trumpet Block
30 × 30cm (12 × 12in)
Three Trumpets with the open end facing outward; one with open end to centre. Free-motion quilted.
Jennie Rayment

Trumpet Sampler
*53 × 53cm (21 × 21in)
Twelve ways to twiddle a
Trumpet.*

Innovative ways to manipulate a Trumpet

(Follow the photograph clockwise from the centre of the sampler)

- Lift and open out. Flatten into a 'kite' shape. Secure corners and roll all edges.

- Insert a small triangle of contrasting-coloured fabric; tuck one side into the Trumpet pocket; roll the folded edges over the other two raw sides of the inserted triangle.

- Insert a contrasting fabric and a Somerset Patch into pocket. Bring lower sides of the Trumpet together; secure with a small vertical bar-tack.

- Pull Trumpet off-centre and insert a Baltimore Rosebud.

- Pleat one side.

- Sew an extra seam in the Trumpet (like a dart). Open out and flatten; pull back edge of the top section.

- Fold over edge of Trumpet (as if turning a collar down). Stitch in place.

- Pull one side across to touch the other side.

- Flatten, pull back edge and insert Baltimore Rosebud.

- Flatten and fold the sides inward to touch; secure then roll other edges.

- Flatten and pull edge back; secure then roll other edges outwards.

- Flatten and pull the top edge back to form a triangle; fold triangle towards top of the Trumpet; open the folds.

Stitching in place

Secure the folds and rolled edges of the Trumpets with a few small stitches. (More stitching might be advisable on any item that receives frequent handling.)

By hand: A small slip or hem stitch is a good choice. Sew through all the layers (a thimble may be required).

By machine: A 90/14 (heavy-duty) needle is preferable, as there are several layers. Use a very short stitch length or several stitches on the spot to catch the folds in place. (The 'fix' setting on some machines is useful for this operation.)

The rolled edges can be held with different machine stitches: such as a straight stitch close to the folded edge, but be careful – it's easy to wobble! Use a narrow zigzag or another decorative pattern instead. Test the design first on a layered pad of fabric, as some of the more complex stitch designs distort when sewing over thick layers.

In my opinion the Blind Hem stitch (page 11) is the best option for anchoring folds or appliquéing edges of Trumpets.

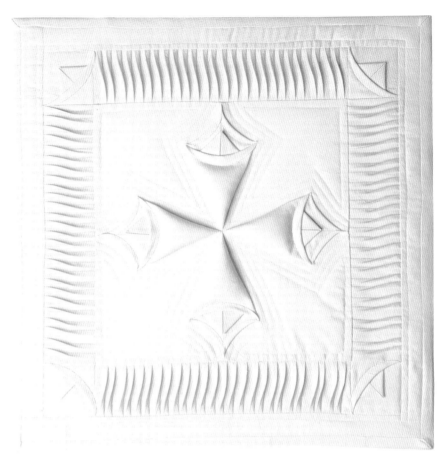

Create a Trumpet block

(See pages 101–105 for the piecing techniques for all the Trumpet block designs.)

A quick and easy textured quilt block can be made from eight squares of the same size.

To make one 30cm (12in) finished block:
Seam allowance: 1cm (⅜in)

Cut eight 17cm (6¾in) squares.

To make one 25cm (10in) finished block
Seam allowance: 1cm (⅜in)

Cut eight 14.5cm (5¾in) squares.

Four squares are used for the Trumpets and four form the background. Why not have the four Trumpets in one colour and the background four another?

Tip: *Because of the many layers, the seams in a Trumpet block are bulky. It is worth reducing some of the bulk by trimming the corner from the Trumpet square prior to folding it. Be careful when using thin or lightly coloured materials because the trimmed edge may show through the top layer.*

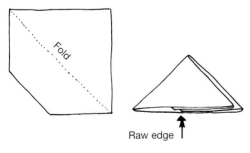

Once trimmed, fold into a triangle for a Trumpet with the raw edge inside.

Construct four Trumpets as described on page 64. Follow page 101 'Four Sections in four squares' for piecing instructions.

Before sewing the two halves of the block together (Stage 7, page 101), think about the design. Which way round will you have the Trumpets? Will all the shapes face the same way (open end to outer edge or vice versa)? What other combinations can be arranged? Try having three Trumpets with the pointed end to centre and one turned the opposite way (see photograph on page 64).

Exploring the design potential

In addition to all the suggestions for innovative manipulation on page 65, why not try the following suggestions?

- Embellish the design with beads, sequins or buttons stitched on the junctions between the shapes. Add a little hand or machine embroidery in relevant places. If the junction of all the seams at the centre of the block is a trifle awry, cover it up with a button!

- How about padding the Trumpets with some little bits of wadding/batting before rolling back the folded edge and sewing in place? Push the filling down firmly before stitching. Padding adds a pleasing three-dimensional effect (see photograph above) to the ultimate design, but don't over-fill the Trumpet.

Calico Trumpets
50 × 50cm (20 × 20in)
Padded Trumpets with Somerset Patch inserts. Tucked border with folded squares and Somerset Patch inserts on corners. Free-motion machine quilted. Mounted on board for easy hanging.
Jennie Rayment

Blue Quilt
*66 × 66cm (26 × 26in)
Trumpets (open end facing
outwards) framed with
folded squares rolled back
into arc. Somerset Patches
inserted under rolled edge.
Crossed-Over Tucks border
with Sharon Square inserts.
Origami corners. Free-
motion machine quilting.
Jennie Rayment*

- Create two-tone Trumpets by sewing two triangles together to make a square. Stitch the triangles on the bias edge; trim seam and press well. When this is folded into a Trumpet and flattened, one colour will be on the outside and one on the inside. Amazing!

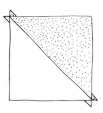 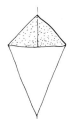

- Take this idea a stage further and make the Trumpet out of three triangles. Now the Trumpet will have one colour inside with a two-tone exterior. If this colour arrangement lacks appeal, refold the Trumpet the other way and the reverse will happen.

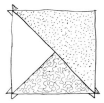 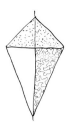

- For further textural creativity, cut four more squares the same size as the others. Fold these diagonally in half and frame the block (align all the raw edges). Roll back the diagonal folded edge of each of the sections to create an arced border.

- Alternatively, secure the centre of each folded square first – stitch through all the layers, then roll back both sides. This makes a very pretty scalloped edging for the Trumpet block.

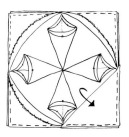

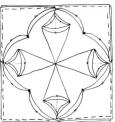

● Change the overall appearance by arranging the Trumpets on the diagonal. Cut a large square into four triangles and arrange the Trumpets on the diagonal as shown in 'Trumpets Rule OK' on page 127.

For a 30cm (12in) finished block
Seam allowance: 1cm (⅜in)

Cut one 33.5cm (13⅛in) square; divide into four triangles. Make Trumpets from four more squares; the size of these squares is your choice, but they must be smaller than 20cm (8in) including any S/A. Follow 'Four Sections – in four triangles' piecing directions as described on page 103. The Trumpets can be placed whichever way round you fancy, and why stop at a square with four inserted Trumpets – what about eight?

Eight Trumpets in a Square

Finished size: 30 × 30cm (12 × 12in)
Seam allowance: 1cm (⅜in)

1. Cut eight 14.5cm (5¾in) squares for Trumpets and four 18.5cm (7⅛in) squares for the background colour.

2. Trim the corner of the Trumpets to reduce bulk before folding and basting as described on page 66.

3. Cut all four background squares diagonally, making eight triangles.

Design 1: Trumpet Cracker
This first appeared as one of the patterns in my Kaleidoscopes 'Block of the Month' Quilt.

Simply Quilts (Show 651)
72 × 72cm (28 × 28in)
Trumpets (open end outwards). Tucked border. Second border embellished with Fancy Fandangos. Baltimore Rosebuds inserted under Fandangos. Machine pieced and free motion quilted. Jennie Rayment

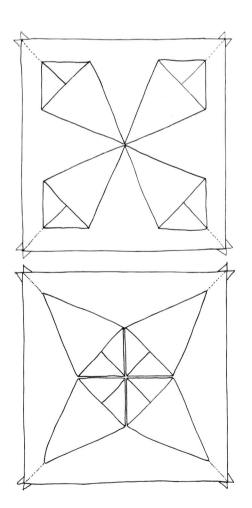

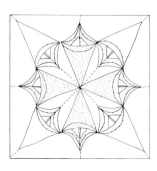

Trumpet Cracker
30 × 30cm (12 × 12in)
Jennie Rayment

1. Lay one Trumpet onto the R/S of one of the triangles, positioning the shape so that the *'two-folded' side* is 4.6cm (1⅞in) from left-hand edge of background square; the single fold will be approximately 3.25 cm (1⅜in) away from the lower/bottom side. *Measure accurately.* Ensure that the raw edges of the Trumpet are exactly in line with the raw diagonal (bias) seam of the triangle underneath. Pin in place.

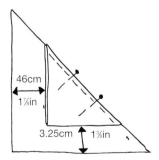

2. Lay a second background triangle on top (right sides together), aligning raw edges. Pin layers.

3. Sew the diagonal side (bias) of triangle using 1cm (⅜in) S/A – regular stitch length; try not to stretch the bias edge while stitching. Remove any basting. Open all the layers in the seam and press well.

4. Flatten the inserted Trumpet into a 'kite' shape; pin in place. Repeat three more times to make four *identical* squares.

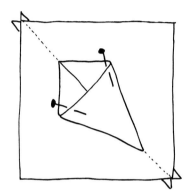

5. Join these four squares together, adding the remaining four Trumpets in the seams. Follow the instructions on page 101. *The open end of these four Trumpets faces away from the centre.*

6. Lift up the last four Trumpets and open out; with a little bit of jiggling and juggling all the pieces will touch as shown in the photograph. Failing this, try a good tweak!

7. Complete the effect by cutting eight 7.5cm (3in) squares; fold these into Somerset Patches (page 50) and tuck into the tops of the Trumpets. Stitch in place.

But how about altering the design?

- Remake the block and turn all the Trumpets round the other way, i.e. openings to the centre (top photograph). Manipulate the Trumpets in different ways.

- Try four Trumpets with openings to the centre and four facing the other way (lower photograph).

- See what other combinations, shapes, forms or diverse designs can be created with some twiddled, twitched and tweaked Trumpets!

Design 2: Trumpet Flower

1. Use the same cutting instructions as Trumpet Cracker and follow the Eight Sections piecing technique as described on page 103.

2. Trim these Trumpets to reduce bulk (see page 66) before inserting them in the seams. In addition, *place the Trumpets with the open end facing the outer edge.* (It is possible to stitch the block with the Trumpets facing the other way, but they will overlap when flattened and the centre section of the seam becomes extremely bulky.)

3. On completion open all the Trumpets, flatten into 'kite' shapes, anchor shapes at the corners and roll back folds. If preferred, the design can be manipulated in many different ways – just have a play and see what happens. Embellish the block with a few buttons and beads.

Trumpet Cracker Variations
30 × 30 cm (12 × 12in)
Somerset Patches inserted.
Machine-pieced and quilted on wadding.
Jennie Rayment

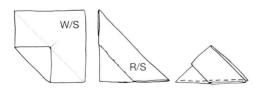

Orange and Green!
80 × 80cm (32 × 32in)
Novel Variation Trumpets
with Somerset Patch and
Baltimore Rosebud inserts.
Free-motion machine
quilting.
Jennie Rayment

A novel variation on the theme

Create a Trumpet with even more manipulative possibilities – another fold to twiddle!

1. Cut the same sized squares as described for 'Eight Trumpets in a Square' – page 68.

2. Press the Trumpets in half diagonally. Fold on the other diagonal and gently finger-press the centre of the square.

3. On the W/S, fold one corner to the centre crease. Refold the Trumpet R/S out with the folded edge on the outside.

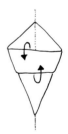

4. Make up the Eight Section block (page 103). Flatten the Trumpets into 'kite' shapes. An extra fold lies across the kite shape.

5. Roll back this fold as far as possible. Why not pull the top edge of the open end of the Trumpet to touch?

6. The shape can be manipulated in many ways; with or without an insert such as a Somerset Patch or a Baltimore Rosebud (pages 50–51) tucked under the new fold and/or in the pocket of the Trumpet.

How about adding more colour?

Make the original Trumpet squares from two different coloured triangles. Use fabrics with no obvious R/S such as plains or hand-dyes. Fabrics with a distinct R/S have to be sewn with one triangle R/S out to the W/S of the other triangle – you will soon find out why! (Try the theory in paper first – it is more economical.)

Using Trumpets

Trumpets can be inserted into any seam and made any size. The variations are endless.

- Insert a Trumpet into a square and use on the corner (see photograph on page 82).

- Arrange several Trumpets in a fan as in 'Orange and Green!' (see photograph on page 71).

- Mix and match Trumpets with other textured shapes, e.g. four Trumpets and four Inserted Squares or Triangles as shown on the next page.

- How about using Trumpets inserted into a seam instead of appliquéd flowers for a pleasing quilt block design?

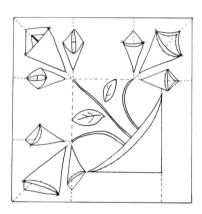

Use your imagination and play – nothing like a bit of Trumpet twiddling to while away a pleasant hour or two.

Create innovative borders

- Alternate the direction of the Trumpets.

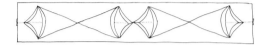

- Tuck one Trumpet into the other as in Prairie Points (page 52).

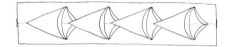

- Cut squares into triangles and insert a Trumpet on the diagonal seam.

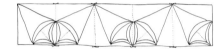

- Alter sizes of the Trumpets and slot into each other in the seam.

All of the above may require a bit of jiggling to get them in the exact place, *but* a judiciously placed button or two would look brilliant.

Black and White
170 × 170cm (67 × 67in)
Trumpets mixed with Inserted
Squares and Triangles.
Blocks bordered with Bias
Strips. Outer Border created
from Trumpets and Inserted
Rectangles. Free-motion
machine quilting.
Jennie Rayment

INSERTED AND MANIPULATED SHAPES

Manipulated squares, right-angled triangles and rectangles form fascinatingly fantastic creations. Arrange these shapes in a square for quilt block designs; insert into a circle; place end to end or side by side in a seam or seams for borders or long panels. Creativity flourishes in abundance with a wealth of fiddling and twiddling and doubtless a few nips and tucks as well. Sounds so good!

The basic construction is elementary: the square or triangle is folded in half, seamed down one edge and turned R/S out; the rectangle is simply folded in half. Then the shapes are inserted into a seam (sandwiched) and can be manipulated into intriguing three-dimensional sculptures.

Crisply finished light- or medium-weight materials are a good choice. Plain materials, hand dyes and self-patterned fabrics are preferable to very ornamental designs; these tend to obscure the manipulated effect. Stripes are most effective, but be very careful to cut the stripes out accurately and fold every piece in the same direction. Avoid directional or pictorial designs.

Inserted Squares

1. Cut a square and fold in half diagonally (R/S together).

2. Sew down one edge using 0.75cm (¼in) seam. Clip the point off seam; flatten into a 'kite' shape and press seam open; turn R/S out and gently poke the point out.

3. Baste the raw edges together using the longest stitch length, keeping the stitching close to the raw edges. Baste from seam towards the point.

4. Insert the shape into a seam (sandwich it). Lift, pull both sides apart and flatten. Amazingly, it turns into a diamond. *The diamond extends beyond the base of the shape.*

5. Before manipulating, fold the diamond in half and press the underside carefully. The section underneath forms a right angle. Fold the flap back to form the diamond shape and press carefully.

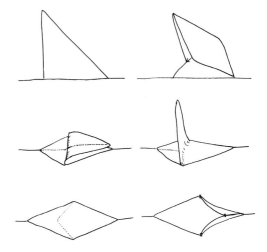

6. All four sides of the diamond are on the bias and can be rolled inwards into arc shapes. The flap of the diamond could be tucked under or twisted in some way. Why not fold the sides of the diamonds to the centre of the shape? This is a very versatile design; experiment a little and see what happens.

7. Once manipulated, secure the shape in relevant places with a few small hand or machine stitches.

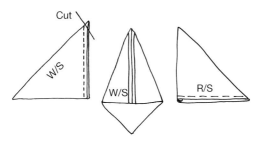

Calico Inserted Squares
74 × 74cm (29 × 29in)
Free-motion machine
quilted on polyester
wadding/batting.
Jennie Rayment

Four Inserted Squares

Finished size: 30 × 30cm (12 × 12in)

Seam allowance: 1cm (⅜in)

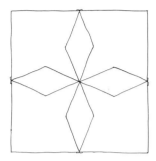

1. For the Inserted Squares, cut four 12cm (4¾in) squares.

2. For the background, cut four 17cm (6¾in) squares.

3. Make up four Inserted Squares (page 75). Follow the 'Four Sections – in four squares' piecing instructions (page 101). The folded (longest) edge faces the centre of the block; the seamed side is to the outer edge.

4. Lift and flatten the shapes before manipulating them. Anchor in place with a few small stitches by hand or machine. A variety of ideas are shown in the photograph on page 75.

5. Complete the block with an arced border: cut four 17cm (6¾in) squares. Fold these into triangles and baste on to the corners. Roll back the folded edges and tuck a Somerset Patch or similar folded shape underneath (page 50).

Four diagonally Inserted Squares

Finished size: 30 × 30cm (12 × 12in) approximately

Seam allowance: 1cm (⅜in)

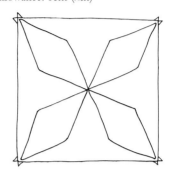

1. For the Inserted Squares, cut four 16cm (6¼in) squares.

2. For the background, cut one 35cm (14in) square. Divide diagonally into four triangles.

3. Make up four Inserted Squares (page 74). Follow the 'Four Sections – in four triangles' piecing instructions (page 103). The folded edge faces the centre of the block, seamed side to the outer edge.

4. Manipulate the Inserted Squares as suggested on page 74, or try the variation described and shown in the photograph below.

A really manipulated Inserted Square
31 × 31cm (12½ × 12½in) Lift shape, flatten into diamond and secure the corners. Raise flap; bring sides together, fold forwards to form a 'sail' sitting on a triangle. Secure both ends of 'sail' with a small stitch. Open and flatten 'sail' into a smaller diamond. Stitch in place through all layers.

Eight Inserted Squares

Finished size: 30 × 30cm (12 × 12in)

Seam allowance: 1cm (⅜in)

1. For the Inserted Squares, cut eight 16cm (6¼in) squares.

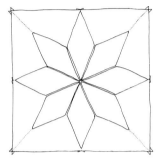

Eight Inserted Squares
31 × 31cm (12½ × 12½in)
Shapes manipulated as
described on page 76.
Sides of Inserted Squares
rolled in arcs. Embellished
with beads.

2. For the background, cut four 18.25cm (7¼in) squares. Divide the squares diagonally into eight triangles.

3. Make up eight Inserted Squares (page 74). Follow the instructions given for 'Eight Sections' (page 103). The folded edge of the Inserted Square faces the centre of the block, seamed side to the outside edge.

4. Pull the sides apart and flatten the shapes into diamonds, and pin in place before pressing. The shapes should touch, although a good tweak may be necessary. Secure the shapes at the corners before rolling back the bias edges to reveal a petal-shaped space.

• For a different arrangement, don't flatten the Inserted Square into a diamond – keep as a triangle. Now, fold the triangle in half lengthways, with the long edge of the triangle underneath.

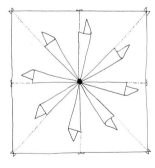

• On completion, add a button or bead in the centre to create a focal point. This extra embellishment conceals most admirably any inadvertent misalignment of the centre seams. Buttons are so useful!

Inserted Squares in a circle

This makes a truly ingenious and effective manipulated and textural creation – an ideal block for a stunning quilt or hanging; the manipulative possibilities are legion. However, drafting a circle with 30°, or 22½° or 18° divisions containing twelve, sixteen or twenty Inserted Squares requires a basic understanding of geometry and careful construction of accurate templates. Is there an easier way?

Template-free – cheating method

Finished size: 46 × 46cm (18 × 18in) approximately
Seam allowance: 0.75cm (¼in)

1. For the Inserted Squares, cut twelve 14.5cm (5¾in) squares.

2. For the background, cut one 56cm (22in) circle.

3. Make up twelve Inserted Squares (page 74).

4. Find the centre of circle by folding in half and half again. Mark the centre. Divide and mark the circle in twelve 30° sections (use a protractor). Rule lines across the fabric through the centre and each 30° mark. Draw a 7cm (2¾in) radius circle in the centre and cut out.

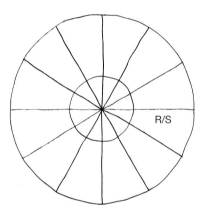

Inserted Squares in a Circle
45 × 45cm (18 × 18in)
Applied thread on centre.
Bias bound. Top stitching
with walking foot.
Jennie Rayment

5. Cut on the lines to make twelve wedge-shaped sections. Label each section on the R/S before cutting to avoid confusion when piecing. (Small adhesive labels are ideal.)

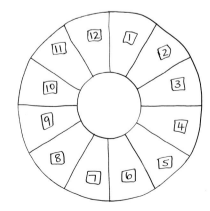

6. Join all the wedge pieces together in the correct order, enclosing one Inserted Square in each seam. Align all the raw edges. Keep the long folded edge of the Inserted Square towards the centre. Sew *an accurate 0.75cm (¼in) seam.* Handle the sections carefully to avoid stretching. The tip of each Inserted Square is aligned with inner corner of the wedge (seam towards outside edge).

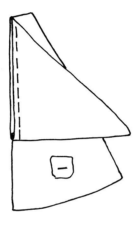

7. Join in pairs first, and then join the pairs into sets of four.

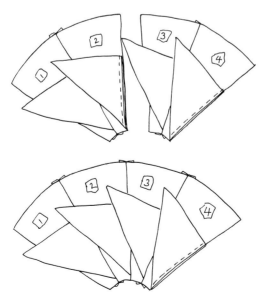

8. Join the three sets together. Pin the Inserted Squares away from the seam when joining all the sections together.

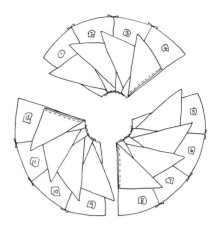

9. Finally, remove the basting and labels, open all the seams and press flat. Stabilize the centre by placing a scrap of material underneath the circle. Pin and baste in place. To complete the centre follow Tucked Circles (page 38).

10. Lift up the Inserted Squares, open out and flatten them into diamonds. All the pieces should touch at corners, but tweak firmly if necessary. Secure the corners with a few small stitches.

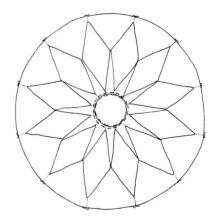

Tip: *If the pieces fail to touch, the answer is a bead at the junctions or dare I say it again…a button!*

● For a small quilt, hanging or tablemat, mount the circle on wadding and a backing fabric. Turn the raw edges under or bind with a bias strip. Before stitching the edge, insert a frill or some other form of embellishment.

- The circle can be applied to another piece of material with Somerset Patches or other folded squares tucked under the edge. After appliquéing, reduce the layers by cutting the fabric away from the underside of the circle before adding any backing.

Design idea
Cut a much larger circle at the start and use the same sized Inserted Squares. Follow the piecing instructions previously described. Add Somerset Patches round the edge.

Calico Circle of Inserted Squares
57 × 57cm (22½ × 22½in)
Bias bound with Babies in Baskets (page 53).
Embellished with beads.
Free-motion quilting.
Jennie Rayment

'Sunflower' in a square

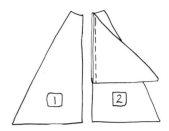

Why make a circle? How about a square block design with overlapped Inserted Squares in different sizes? (See Sunflowers on page 125.)

Finished size: 35 × 35cm (14 × 14in) approximately

Seam allowance: 0.75cm (¼in)

1. For the Inserted Squares, cut eight 13cm (5¼in) squares and eight 11cm (4½in) squares.

2. For the background, cut one 46cm (18in) square.

3. Construct all sixteen Inserted Squares. Keep the two different sizes separated.

4. Fold the background square into four to find the centre. Mark the centre. Use a protractor and divide into sixteen 22½° sections. Rule lines across the fabric through every degree mark. Set the compass at 7.5cm (3in) radius and draw a circle in the centre. Cut out the circle. Label each section before cutting every line. Cut into sixteen wedges.

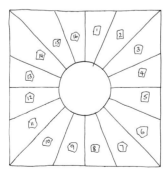

5. Stitch the wedges into *pairs,* including *one larger 13cm (5¼in) Inserted Square in each seam.* Ensure that the tip of the Inserted Square is exactly at the tip of the wedge. Align all the raw edges. Keep the long folded edge towards the centre. Look at the diagram carefully.

6. Make eight sets. Sew all eight sets together with *one smaller 11cm (4½in) Inserted Square in* these seams. (The larger squares are alternated with the smaller ones.)

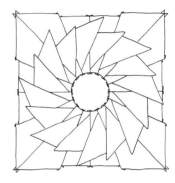

7. Follow Tucked Circle (page 39, Stage 12 onwards) for instructions on making and applying the centre. Trim the edges of the design level when completed.

8. Lift the Inserted Squares and flatten into diamonds. Overlap the smaller diamonds over the larger ones, or vice versa. Manipulate the shapes as desired and secure in place with a few small stitches.

Inserted Triangles

Use right-angled triangles instead of squares to produce subtly different shapes and create a variety of unusual textured blocks and border designs. *Unlike Inserted Squares, when flattened this shape does not extend beyond its base.*

The simplest way to cut a right-angled triangle is to divide a square diagonally in half and *voilà!*…two triangles.

1. Fold one triangle in half and stitch down the bias (stretchy) edge using 0.75cm (¼in) S/A. Clip the point off the seam.

2. Flatten the shape into a square and press the seam open.

3. Turn R/S out and rearrange into a triangle. Baste the raw edges; start from the seam and sew towards the point, using the longest stitch length and keeping the stitching close to the raw edges.

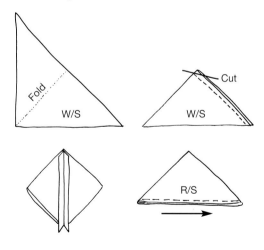

4. This shape is now inserted (sandwiched) into a seam. To manipulate, lift the shape and pull the sides apart. It flattens into a diamond with a small right-angled flap. The flap can be turned either way, revealing more or less of the seam. The edges are on the bias and can be rolled as in the photograph.

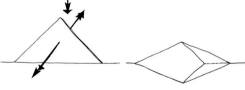

Design ideas

The Inserted Triangle does not have to be flattened into a diamond; see what you can create. Flatten it to the side, squash it, roll into a cone, tuck the flap inside or bring the sides together.

Many of the ideas for manipulating Inserted Squares can be used for Inserted Triangles, as can the piecing techniques. For instance: sandwich the Inserted Triangle in four squares, four triangles, in circles or indeed anywhere you like. For a novel hexagonal design, sandwich six Inserted Triangles between six equilateral (60°) triangles – the shapes will not touch each other but an interesting effect will be created.

Eight Inserted Triangles with textured borders
64 × 64cm (25 × 25in)
Tucks and Bias Strip borders. Trumpets inserted in corners. Calico (muslin in USA) and batik. Machine pieced and free-motion quilted.
Jennie Rayment

Eight Inserted Triangles
30 × 30cm (12 × 12in)
Microwave-dyed calico
Inserted Triangles with
calico background. A free-
machine embroidered
flower in centre.
Jennie Rayment

Eight Inserted Triangles in a square

Why not make a starry quilt block using Inserted Triangles? Use different colours for the shapes or create the design in monochrome.

Finished size: 30 × 30cm (12 × 12in)

Seam allowance: 1cm (⅜in)

1. For the Inserted Triangles, cut four 16cm (6¼in) squares; cut in half to form eight triangles.

2. For the background, cut four 18.25cm (7¼in) squares; cut in half to form eight triangles.

3. Construct the Inserted Triangles as described on page 82. Make up the block by following the instructions given in 'Eight Sections' (page 103). The folded edge of the Inserted Triangle faces the centre of the block, the seamed side to the outside.

Tip: *Should your sample fail to resemble the diagrams on page 103, turn the Inserted Triangle to the other side – it can lie on* either *side of seam.*

4. Try a little manipulation when the construction is complete. Lift the shapes, pull the sides apart and flatten into diamonds. The diamonds should touch and be of equal size. Pleasingly, the sides of the Inserted Triangles are on the bias so they can be tweaked or even tugged firmly into place. Choose whether the small triangular flap faces the centre of the block or away. Pin all the shapes in place before pressing.

5. Secure the corners of the diamonds before rolling any edges. (Should they fail to touch, beads at the junctions can be very effective.)

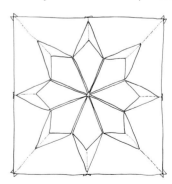

● On completion, this particular design really needs a button in the centre for a focal point to create the optimum impact of dynamic design (sounds so professional!). Bigger buttons are better and cunningly cover any little inadvertent glitches in the piecing splendidly.

Calico Concoction
155 × 155cm (61 × 61in)
Inserted Triangles and
Trumpet blocks – some of
the Trumpets are padded.
Two tucked borders and
one Crossed-Over Tucks
border. Free-motion quilted.
Jennie Rayment

Mixing inserted shapes in a square

- Combine four Inserted Squares with four Trumpets. Cut all eight squares the same size; fold four into Trumpets and make four Inserted Squares (see photograph on page 84).

- Combine four Inserted Triangles and four Inserted Squares for an innovative design.

Have a play and see what happens.

Borders with Inserted Squares and Triangles

The epitome of originality – designer borders with Inserted Squares or Triangles.

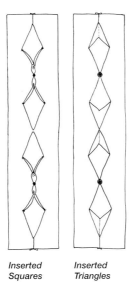

Inserted   Inserted
Squares   Triangles

The shapes are placed end to end in a seam with beads at the junctions.

For even more really dynamically intriguing pieced border designs, arrange the shapes diagonally.

1. Cut squares for the background; divide these diagonally into triangles.

2. Piece these triangles together to form squares with an Inserted Square/Triangle sandwiched in each seam.

Why not increase the potential for textural twiddling by including a Trumpet or two when the squares are stitched together? See the Textured Sampler Quilt on page 6. Creativity rules OK and if the pieces don't meet, embellish with buttons, beads or even bows.

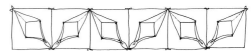

Background squares with Inserted Triangles

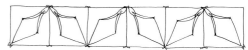

Background squares with Inserted Squares

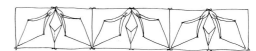

Background squares with Inserted Squares and Triangles

Background squares with Inserted Squares with Trumpets

Yellow and Green
60 × 60cm (24 × 24in)
Centre Block: Inserted
Squares and Triangles.
Border: Two different sized
Inserted Rectangles
overlapped in seam. Folded
squares on corners with
Baltimore Rosebuds tucked
inside. Machine pieced and
quilted.
Jennie Rayment

Inserted Rectangles

This is a different concept from the other techniques described in this chapter, as the rectangle is not stitched beforehand but is folded in half and then inserted in a seam. Once inserted it is opened out and flattened to form a right-angled triangle, although there are other permutations.

The Inserted Rectangle may be used for attractive textured borders, blocks or as a textural embellishment. The sides of the shape are on the bias and roll to form gentle curves. In addition, beneath the shape there is a little pocket...another textured titbit could be tucked in, or whatever else you fancy.

Unlike the Inserted Square and Triangle, after the rectangle has been inserted and opened to form a triangle, there is still a raw edge; consequently the rectangle should be placed at the end of a seam, then the next seam will cover this raw edge.

To achieve an accurate triangular shape, the sides of the rectangle need to be in proportion. The length is twice the width, i.e. 6 × 3, 8 × 4, 10 × 5, etc. This applies to both imperial and metric measurements (remember to add seam allowances).

An Inserted Rectangle can be included in any seam. Sandwiching a rectangle between two squares makes an eminently suitable unit for blocks or borders. (The squares are the same size as the width of the rectangle plus relevant seam allowances.) Sew several of these units together, roll back the folds and hey presto! a scalloped edging.

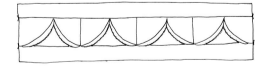

Inserted Rectangles border

For a 7.5cm (3in) wide border

This border is suitable for any length divisible by 15cm (6in).
Seam allowance: 0.75cm (¼in)

1. Divide the length of the border by 15cm (6in) to calculate how many units are required. Cut *one* rectangle and *two* squares for each unit.

2. For the Rectangles, cut fabric 16.5 × 9cm (6½ × 3½in).

3. For the Squares, cut 9cm (3½in) squares.

3. Fold one Rectangle in half, R/S out, forming a 9 × 8.25cm (3½ × 3¼in) shape.

4. Place this on one 9cm (3½in) square (R/S up), aligning the folded edge of the rectangle, exactly 0.75cm (¼in) from top of the square; match raw edges; pin in place.

5. Lay another square on top, 'sandwiching' the rectangle. Stitch the pinned side of the rectangle, using 0.75cm (¼in) S/A.

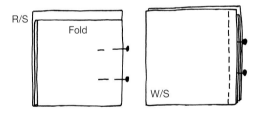

6. Turn section to W/S, open the entire seam and press, flattening the little 'nose' at the top of the inserted rectangle. Press the seam only; try not to crease the rectangle.

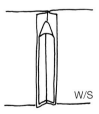

7. Make the correct number of units as required for the length of the border.

The next stage is different from the one described in my other books.

8. Join all the units together forming a long strip, leaving the rectangles unopened. Press seams open and flat.

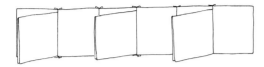

9. On completion, open the rectangles, pull the two corners of the rectangle apart and flatten the shape. Amazingly there is a triangle! Carefully arrange these triangles so that the corners overlap on the seam, i.e. 0.75cm (¼in) from the edge. Pin and baste close to the raw edge.

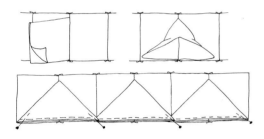

Tip: *It is preferable to attach the border to the quilt/ hanging etc. or to cover the raw edges with another strip before rolling the folded sides of the triangles into arcs. If this is not done, the rolled edge may get caught in the next seam.*

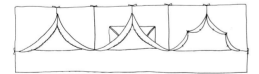

10. Roll the edge in a complete scallop, or secure the mid-point of the folded edge to the background square then roll both sides to form a double scallop. For more textural interest, tuck a folded square of some sort into the pocket beneath the triangle. Stitch in place by hand or machine (see Blind Hem Stitch, page 11).

For a 15cm (6in)-wide border

This is suitable for any length divisible by 7.5cm (3in).

Seam allowance: 0.75cm (¼in)

1. Calculate how many units are required by dividing the length of the border by 7.5cm (3in).

2. Cut one rectangle and two squares for each unit in the same sizes as suggested on page 87.

3. Follow Stages 1–7 on page 87, then open and flatten the rectangle into a triangle. Ensure the points of the triangle bisect the corners of the background squares. Pin in place. Be picky – it pays. Baste (inside S/A) the raw edge.

4. Make as many units as required, and stitch together in a row as shown below. Pressing seams open and flat. Guess what – it forms Flying Geese (a traditional patchwork design). The edges of these 'geese' roll and textural inserts can be tucked into the pockets – altogether much more interesting than the usual version of this technique!

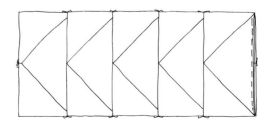

Dutchman's Puzzle &
Flying Geese 60 × 60cm
(24 × 24in)
Somerset Patches and
coloured inserts in the
Flying Geese. Free-motion
machine quilted.
Jennie Rayment

5. For accurate piecing, sew the sections together with the 'nose' side up. The tip of the 'nose' is the top of the triangle on the R/S.

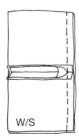

6. Stitch across the top of the 'nose', then the point of the triangle should be precise on the R/S. A subtle deviation (wiggle) to the designated seam allowance may be necessary for an accurate design!

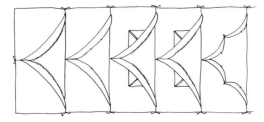

7. Roll back the folded edges in a scallop. For a double scallop, secure the midpoint and/or tuck in some form of embellishment.

Experiment with the design

•   Flying Geese do not have to point in the same direction; they can fly any which way. Why not reverse the shapes in the centre of the band?

•   Reverse two Geese (back to back) to make a square. Lay another piece of fabric in the centre of this square and roll the edges over (similar to a Cathedral Window – traditional patchwork design).

Why not make a square quilt block?

•   Use these sections to make the Dutchman's Puzzle (a traditional patchwork design). Make eight units and sew together as shown in the centre panel of the photograph. Vary the design by cutting some of the background squares in a different colour.

•   For added manipulated impact, roll the folded edges of the triangles and insert a Somerset Patch (page 50) in the pocket beneath.

•   Increase the size and make a small hanging/cot quilt by adding a border of smaller Flying Geese. Place them back to back in the centre of the border and add a coloured insert.

•   Alternatively use this design as the centre of a medallion quilt. (Medallion quilts are a series of borders around a central panel.)

More ideas with Inserted Rectangles

Use the construction method for the 7.5cm (3in) border (page 87).

Vary the sizes of the rectangles

1. Make up the units as described in Stages 1–7 on page 87, but include another rectangle in the seam between each section. This could be smaller than the original ones. Try not to catch the original rectangle in the seam when sewing units together.

2. Open out all the rectangles and overlap one over the other (see photograph on page 86). Pin in place before basting the raw edge.

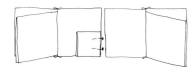

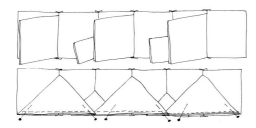

Design idea
A thought…both this diagram and the photograph on page 89 show the smaller rectangle behind the larger one – why not reverse them? Have the smaller shape in front of the larger one – try it and see.

Petal Pattern Border

1. Join the units with another rectangle the same size inserted *the other way up* in the seam between each section.

2. Pin/turn the original rectangles out of the way to prevent them being caught.

3. Open all the rectangles and arrange into triangles. The triangles should touch at the tip

and overlap each other on the seam. Pin and baste both sides of the strip.

4. Roll the folds back to make the 'petal' shapes.

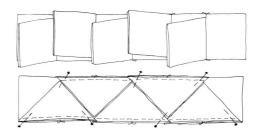

5. To complete the pattern, cut two more squares (same size as the background ones). Fold these diagonally in half. Baste in place.

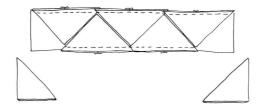

6. Add strips to the outer edges before rolling back all the folds.

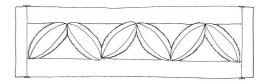

Colour and embellishment potential

- The background squares and the rectangles could be different colours. How about black rectangles and 'colour wash' for the squares?

- Embroider the centre of the 'petal' shape with unusual machine stitches and diverse threads.

- Sew lots of these strips together for a snazzy scrap quilt using all the odd remnants from that precious stash.

Add more folds

- Arrange the Inserted Rectangle as a triangle and fold the corners inwards. Baste the raw edges to hold the layers. Roll back the folds and stitch in place.

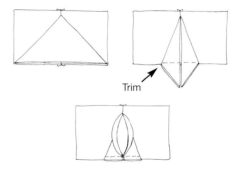

- Or, fold both sides over to touch in the centre. Baste the raw edge and trim. Roll back the folds to form a 'petal' shape.

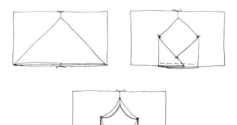

Add more colour

1. Baste the bottom of the triangle. Cut a smaller piece of contrasting-coloured material and lay on top. Pin in place.

2. Attach an extra strip to cover the raw edge before rolling the folds over the raw sides of the contrasting-coloured triangle. Stitch in place (the Blind Hem stitch, page 11, is ideal).

Make a mock Cathedral Window block

The completed design resembles the Secret Garden version of Cathedral Windows (a traditional patchwork design).

Use the construction method for the 15cm (6in) border, page 88.

1. Make two units (remember to baste the raw edge) and cut two more rectangles.

2. Fold the rectangles in half and lay both of them on one of the units, butting the folded edges at the centre. Pin in place. Sew both units together (points of triangles to centre).

3. Open out the last pair of rectangles, and flatten them into triangles. All the triangles should touch on the diagonals. Baste the remaining raw edges.

4. Roll back the folds to create four petal-shaped spaces. Add a decorative touch with some buttons or beads at the centre.

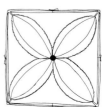

Border designs with Inserted Rectangles

- Join the Inserted Rectangle units with a Trumpet (see Textured Sampler Quilt, page 6) or an Inserted Square in each seam. (The Trumpets/Inserted Squares should be cut to the same length or shorter than the background squares.)

- For an interesting textured border, cut squares and sew together with two folded rectangles (folded edges butted together) in each seam. (The squares are the same size as the length of the rectangle, e.g. 16.5cm [6½in].) Open the rectangles to form triangles. Baste in place before adding the borders. Roll the edges of the triangles to form arcs, and tuck in Somerset Patches (page 50).

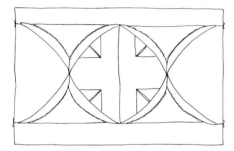

- Create a fascinating frame to a quilt by sewing short strips together with an Inserted Rectangle and a Trumpet in every seam.

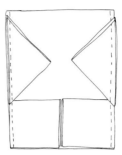

- Open and flatten both the Trumpets and the rectangles. Add a border to cover the raw edges of the Inserted Rectangles before rolling the folds. Manipulate the Trumpets.

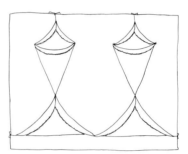

Inserted Rectangles à la Cathedral Window
Bag: 50 × 38cm (20 × 15in)
Cushion: 38 × 38cm (15 × 15in)
Jennie Rayment

BIAS STRIPS

Create a fabulously scintillating border or sashing from two bias-cut strips. The strips are folded and laid on a backing material, stitched in place with large seams forming two wide tucks. The tucks are secured at intervals then rolled back revealing the backing fabric through arc-shaped apertures.

Cutting Bias Strips

Before cutting the Bias Strips, decide on the *finished width*. Add a seam allowance of 0.75cm (¼in) to one side and 2.5cm (1in) to the other, e.g. for a 5cm (2in) finished strip, cut strips 8.25cm (3¼in) wide.

Bias strips can be cut in several ways; here are two of them. Considerable fabric savings can be made with the first method, although some of the pieces will have two or more seams when cut into shorter sections.

'Continuous Bias Binding' technique

1. Cut a large square of material and cut it in half diagonally.

2. Sew both triangles to make a diamond. Press the seam open and flat.

3. On the W/S, rule parallel lines from one side to the other. (Distance between the lines is the desired width of the bias strip *plus S/A*.)

4. Roll into a cylinder (W/S out) aligning **B** & **C**, *not* **A** & **B**. Pin securely in place before sewing the seam.

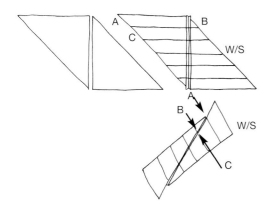

5. Use scissors to cut along the drawn line. Start at **A,** follow the line (the drawn line spirals round the cylinder). Amazingly you will get a continuous strip of material. Press the strip lightly (all edges are bias). Cut into the desired lengths.

Rotary-cut Bias Strips

Begin by calculating the correct width of material needed to obtain Bias Strips of a specific length. (This is less wasteful than cutting Bias Strips of an indeterminate length.) Calculating the width does not require complicated mathematics involving hypotenuses and Pythagoras. No hard sums are needed!

1. On the 45° line on the cutting mat, measure the length of bias strip required. Run your finger horizontally or vertically from the end of this measurement to the edge of the mat. Read off the amount of centimetres/inches (usually marked on the edge). This gives you the required width of the fabric.

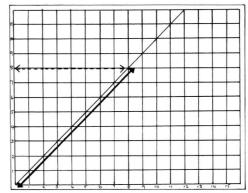

2. Add an extra 5cm (2in) to this figure to compensate for trimming the diagonal end of the bias strip.

3. Cut a width of material to this measurement; open out and lay it flat on the cutting mat.

4. Place the ruler on to the fabric, align the 45° line (marked on ruler) with the selvedge of the material; cut along the edge of ruler.

Kaleidoscopes
*150 × 190cm (60 × 75in)
'Block of the Month' –
twelve different textured
blocks with Bias Strip
borders. Features
Dutchman's Puzzle and
Trumpet Cracker. Hoffman
Batiks. Free-motion
machine quilted.
Jennie Rayment*

5. From this cut edge, measure the width of bias strip required and cut the first strip; continue cutting to the end of the fabric. Trim the ends level and cut into desired lengths.

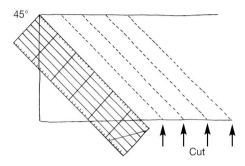

Tip: *To save wastage, cut the leftover triangles (either end) into Bias Strips and join. Trim the seams and press open.*

Tip: *Cut a large number of Bias Strips quickly by layering three to four widths of fabric. Cut all layers simultaneously. A really sharp cutter cuts through 12 layers of fabric easily – given a bit of welly (force)!*

Bias Strip borders

Two Bias Strips are applied to a backing material. All the pieces could be the same colour, or different ones. The backing fabric is revealed when the Bias Strips are rolled back.

Finished width: 10 × 10cm (4 × 4in)

Seam allowance: variable – see text

1. Measure the length of the border: Cut one *straight grain* 5cm (2in) wide strip of backing material this measurement.

2. Cut two 8.25cm (3¼in) wide Bias Strips and trim level to the same measurement.

3. Fold and press 2.5cm (1in) over to the W/S on one long side of each bias strip.

4. Fold the backing strip in half lengthways and finger-press. Butt folded edge of both Bias Strips to centre crease of backing fabric (R/S up); pin in place.

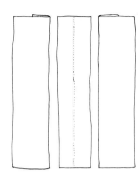

5. Sew a 1.25cm (½in) seam either side of the two centre folds (normal stitch length) forming two wide tucks. Remove pins and open out both tucks.

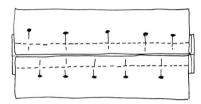

6. Embellish the channel with decorative embroidery stitches in a contrasting colour.

Tip: *Lay a thin piece of paper under the backing fabric to prevent the material buckling when a heavy decorative stitch is sewn. Tear away afterwards. (Tissue, tracing or kitchen paper is adequate, or purchase 'Stitch 'n Tear'.)*

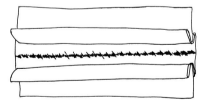

Design ideas
*   Why not use a twin needle and two different coloured threads (one through each eye)? Select a simple pattern and test the stitch width before you start sewing.

*   *Alternatively* appliqué a ribbon or braid down the centre of the channel.

7. Close the tucks. Measure 0.75cm (¼in) from each end of the strip. Secure the tucks with a few small stitches or tiny bar-tack. Divide the remaining space in sections. Make the sections a minimum of 6.5cm (2½in) in length. Stitch the tucks at these points with the same-sized stitching.

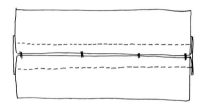

8. Roll back the tucks to reveal the backing strip. Stitch the rolled edge in place by hand or machine. The Blind Hem stitch (page 11) is a

good option, or try any other decorative machine stitch.

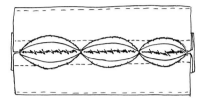

9. Baste the outside edges of the border to prevent the Bias Strips stretching. (Clip the stitching in several places if the fabric bunches. There will still be some stability to the stitched edge even when clipped.)

10. Stitch the border in place using a 0.75cm (¼in) seam.

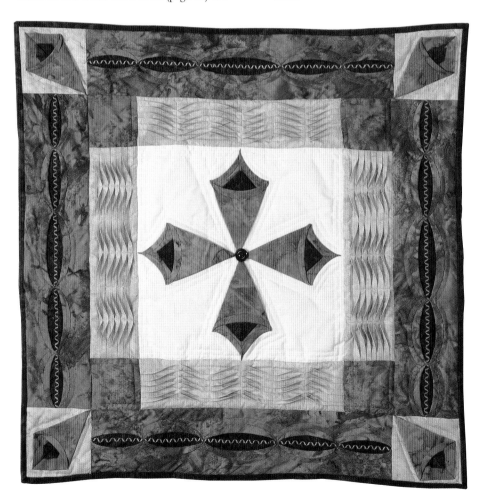

Coming up Trumps
68 × 68cm (27 × 27in) Trumpet block centre with Somerset Patches. Tucked and Bias Strips borders. Trumpets with Baltimore Rosebud inserts on corners. Machine quilted with the walking foot. Monochrome version on page 114. Jennie Rayment

More suggestions

- How about a variety of different colours showing inside the ovals? Join different fabrics to make the backing strip. Adjust the distances between the bar-tacks to fit the changes in colour and cover the seams.

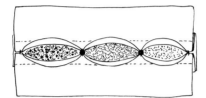

- Striped fabrics and those with directional designs are most effective. Alternatively, select a particular part of a pattern such as a line of flowers, leaves or a specific motif.

- Change the spacing of the bar-tacks and make the oval shapes larger or smaller. Smaller oval shapes can be made but the rolled bias edge is minimized. Larger gaps between the junctions produce a greater roll back. Sometimes more is better than less!

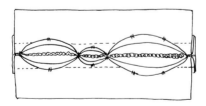

- Don't sew the rolled-back bias tucks down completely – secure in one place only.

- Cover the bar-tacks with beads or some small buttons.

- To create a wider bias arc, increase the width of the seam allowance to 2cm (1⅜in). A wider seam with a longer gap between the bar-tacks creates a greater bias arc.

Extend the principle

- Create a double bias edge by adding another bias strip to either side of the first ones. Stitch this in place using the same seam allowance (1.25cm [½in]), secure the tuck at intervals and roll back. Stitch the rolled edge down. See Textured Sampler quilt on page 6.

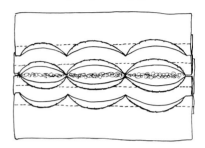

- Or use one bias strip only. An interesting arced edge can be made with one bias strip applied to a background material. Sew a 1.25cm (½in) or wider seam, secure the tuck at selected intervals, roll back the folded bias edge and stitch in place. (See 'Mélange' page 122.)

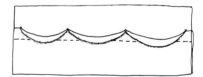

Bias Strip block

Finished size: 30 × 30cm (12 × 12in)

1. Cut one 38cm (15in) strip across the full
    width of the fabric (110cm[44in]). From this
    strip cut five 12cm (5in)-wide Bias Strips. Fold
    and press *both* bias edges over to meet on the
    back (resembles giant bias binding).

2. Cut one 31.5cm (12½in) backing square in the
    same or a contrasting-coloured material. (The
    backing shows when the strips are rolled
    back.) Cover the backing material with the
    pressed Bias Strips. Trim the strips level with
    the backing material. Pin all the layers well.

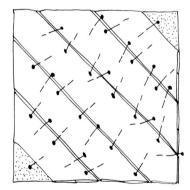

Tip: *At this point the block could be placed on some
batting/wadding to stop the backing fabric distorting
when the bias tucks are rolled.*

3. Sew a 1.25cm (½in) seam along the edge of
    each bias strip. Sew this size of seam easily and
    accurately by moving the needle to the left-
    hand side of the presser foot or by marking
    the fabric.

Tip: *Moving needle: The gap between the needle and
the edge of the presser foot is approximately 1cm (⅜in)
when the needle is moved to the left-hand side of the foot.
Place the edge of the foot 0.25cm (⅛in) from the edge of
the bias tuck. The needle should now be 1.25cm (½in)
from the edge of the tuck. On some models, the needle
can be set exactly 1.25cm (½in) from the presser foot edge.*

Tip: *Marking the seam: Rule a line or score the
fabric – run the point of a stitch ripper, blunt screwdriver,
barbecue skewer or something similar down the edge of
the ruler. (There is a gadget available for scoring fabric
but other devices can be substituted.)*

4. Open the tucks and embellish the channel
    with a decorative machine stitch, hand
    embroidery, ribbon or lace. (Lay thin paper
    under the backing material to prevent the
    fabric distorting when sewing any heavy satin
    stitch design.)

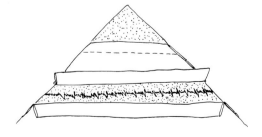

Cushion covers, quilt block and Bias Bob!

These feature a variety of ways to manipulate the Bias Strips.
Jennie Rayment

5. Close the tucks. Stitch the tucks down at 6.5cm (2½in) intervals or more. Sewing parallel lines across the work is the fastest way to anchor the tucks.

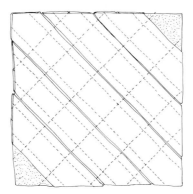

Or anchoring the tucks individually at different distances (by hand or with a very small machine stitch) is another option.

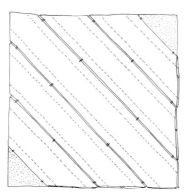

6. Roll back the edges of the bias tucks and stitch in place (page 96).

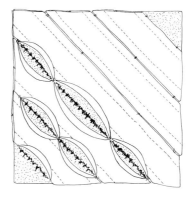

Other variations

● Leave parts of the bias tucks unopened.

● Change the effect completely by catching the bias tucks individually on either side of the channel. Roll one side out completely, catch the other side midway and roll back either side. Resembles lips!

PIECING TECHNIQUES

Many of the blocks in this book contain four or eight inserted sections. These designs are pieced together with a background fabric to form a square and then manipulated. In preference to repeating the construction technique each time, this chapter describes the specific methods for piecing both. Note that the inserted shape may differ but the piecing method is the same.

Seam allowance (S/A) = 1cm (⅜in). This slightly wider seam than the usual 0.75cm (¼in) makes it easier to arrange the inserted sections with their points touching at the centre. Admittedly, a button or some beads in the centre would improve most of the designs and create a focal point. Extra embellishment is not a cop-out but it does disguise an inadvertent misalignment!

Two thoughts to remember:

- Check which side of the inserted shape faces the centre. Failing to get the piece in the correct way could be disastrous. On the other hand, the result could be most unusual.

- Picky people do perfect piecing with precisely positioned points. Does it all really matter?

Cut the correct sizes for each block as stated in the relevant text. If these sizes have to be altered, recalculate the measurements remembering to add 1cm (⅜in) S/A to the background pieces.

See page 9 for advice on setting an accurate 1cm (⅜in) seam on the sewing machine.

Do not panic if your sample fails to resemble the diagrams – turn the shape over to the other side of the seam. The insertion can lie on either side.

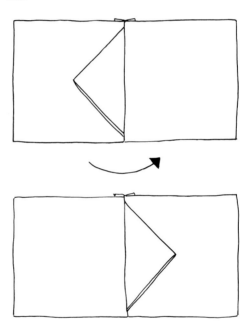

Important: *All the diagrams in this chapter relate to Trumpets, but the inserted section could be any other shape. The method is the same even if the shape is different.*

Four sections – in four squares

Seam allowance: 1cm (⅜in)

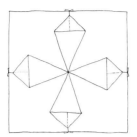

1. Lay one background square R/S up and place one inserted shape on top. Align the tip of the inserted section exactly with the top right-hand corner of the background square; match all the raw edges.

2. The corner at **C** is the centre of the block; check the inserted shape faces the correct way.

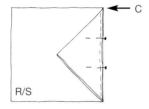

Even if the background square is larger, the inserted section will still be aligned exactly with **C** – the top right-hand corner. (**C** is for centre!)

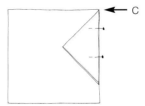

3. Pin the inserted shape in place. Ensure that the piece faces the correct way or the final design might be a little surprising – not quite what was envisaged!

4. Place the other background square on top. Sew a 1cm (⅜in) seam. The inserted shape is now sandwiched between two background squares.

5. Remove any basting before pressing the entire seam open and as flat as possible.

6. Repeat the last stage with one more inserted shape and the last two background squares. Two halves of the finished block are now made and two inserted shapes remain.

7. Open out one of these halves and lay it down with the centre of the block away from you. Place one inserted shape (correct end of shape to centre of block) on right-hand side first, aligning all raw edges. Position the shape carefully – there should be no gaps between this shape and the tip of the previously inserted one at **A**. Pin in place.

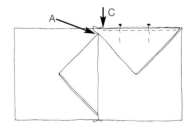

8. Lay the last inserted shape (left-hand side) on top so that it overlaps the right-hand piece at **A** (the very tip of the initially inserted shape) and all the raw edges match. Both inserted shapes must overlap each other at **A** – **A** is for Accuracy. Be picky about the overlap otherwise the shapes may not meet at the centre. Pin the pieces well.

Tip: *Technically, there should be a 1cm (⅜in) gap between **A** (the top of the first inserted shape) and the raw edge; sadly this does not always happen. Murphy's law prevails! Redo the seam a little wider if there is insufficient space to overlap the last two inserted shapes easily. To get all the points to meet in the centre the tips of the shapes have to touch. The next seam will pass through **A** regardless of the designated seam allowance.*

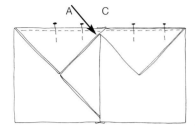

9. Baste the shapes in place before stitching the two halves together. Start the basting just before **A**. (Basting straight across the edge from one side to the other may result in the inserted shapes moving apart in the centre.) In addition, baste through the junction at **A** to ensure that all the pieces are held in place precisely. Complete the basting by turning the work or sew backwards across the remaining part of it.

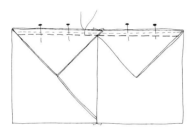

10. Lay the second half on top – turning its inserted section in the opposite direction to the one inserted in the first half. Match up the centre points at **A** and pin well. *Check the inserted shape on the second half faces the correct way.*

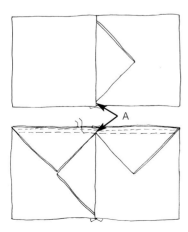

11. Sew the block together with the basted side uppermost. Follow the basting line (basting passes through the junction at **A**). The seam should also pass across the top of the first inserted shape. Use a larger machine needle and increase the stitch length slightly. The seam ought to be 1cm (⅜in); but it is much more important to sew through the junction of all the points at **A**.

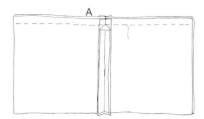

12. Remove the basting and press the seam open as much as possible before manipulating the inserted shapes as desired.

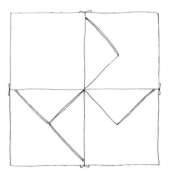

Tip: *If the tips of the inserted shapes do not meet exactly in the centre, minor glitches or hiccups can be concealed with small buttons, beads or a few French or Bullion Knots. Major glitches just require bigger buttons!*

Four sections – in four triangles

Seam allowance: 1cm (⅜in)

Joining four triangles with an inserted section in the diagonal seams creates quite a difference in the appearance of the block. In addition, the inserted pieces can be cut larger than those pieced between four squares.

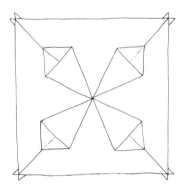

Cut the background square diagonally into four sections. Follow the same piecing technique as described in the previous section, i.e. make two halves, put right-hand side section in place first, then left-hand etc. Watch the overlap at **A**.

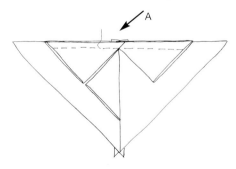

Tip: *If your sample fails to resemble any of the diagrams, turn the shape to the other side – the insertion can lie on either side of seam. And…take care that the inserted shapes are facing the right direction. It is so easy to get it wrong.*

Eight sections

Seam allowance: 1cm (⅜in)

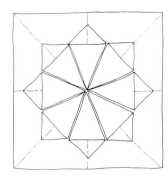

1. Cut four background squares diagonally in half to form eight triangles. Make eight inserted shapes and baste if needed. (Trumpets should be trimmed inside to reduce the seam bulk.)

2. Lay one background triangle, R/S up, and place one inserted shape on top. *The top of the background triangle **C** is the centre of the block.* Place the shape 1cm (⅜in) from the straight side of the triangle with all the raw edges aligned exactly on the bias edge. Check that the inserted piece is facing the correct way. Pin in place. (For accurate and speedy measuring, cut a 1cm (⅜in)-wide strip of paper or card and use this as the guide.)

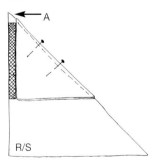

Tip: *Setting the shape 1cm (⅜in) from the raw edge allows sufficient space at its tip for the next seam. This measurement is directly related to the seam allowance i.e. 1cm (⅜in). Should the seam allowance need adjusting for some reason, then place the shape at the adjusted S/A from the raw edge. Failure to set the shape in by the specific seam allowance may result in its tip being sewn into the next set of seams.*

3. Take a second background triangle and place on top (R/S together). Align the raw edges and pin the layers together. Sew a 1cm (⅜in) seam down the diagonal side (bias) of triangle, using the regular stitch length (2–2.5mm). Try not to stretch the bias edge while stitching.

4. Repeat Stages 1–2 and make four *identical* squares.

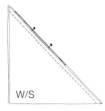

5. Remove any basting. Open all layers in the seam and press flat to reduce bulk. *Press two sets with the inserted shape to the right and two sets with the inserted shape to the left.* (Pressing the pieces this way prevents the shapes catching in the seam when these squares are joined.)

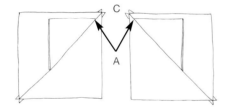

6. Take one left-hand pressed square and place one more inserted shape on top, aligning its tip with the top of the background square. This next piece must touch the first one at **A**. (**A** should be 1cm (⅜in) from the raw edge *but* whatever distance **A** is from the raw edge will now be the seam allowance.) Check the inserted shape faces the correct way. **C** is the centre.

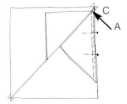

7. Match the raw edges. Pin and baste through **A** to hold the inserted shape accurately in place.

8. Lay one right-hand pressed square on top (R/S together): both diagonal seams point to centre of block **C**. Stitch the two squares together, matching the diagonal seams carefully. Sew the seam from the centre out. A wooden skewer (page 13) is excellent for holding the layers steady as you commence stitching.

9. Open out, remove basting and press seams open and flat. Repeat this stage using the other two pressed squares and one more inserted shape. Trim the 'ears' flush with the seam allowances. Both halves of the block are now complete and there are two inserted shapes left.

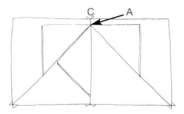

10. Take one of these halves, turn the inserts away from the last seam, and pin. (This prevents the shapes catching in the next seam.)

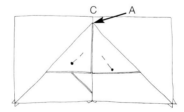

11. Place one more inserted section (correct end of shape to centre of block) on right-hand side first, aligning all raw edges. Position the shape carefully – there must be *no gap* at **A** between this shape and the top of the other inserted shapes. Pin.

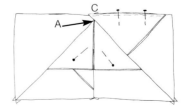

12. Lay the last inserted shape (left-hand side) on top overlapping the right-hand piece at **A** – make sure that it overlaps precisely – there should be no gaps. (Technically these last two pieces should overlap 1cm (⅜in) from the raw edge, but may not; those little gremlins again!) Align all raw edges and pin.

13. Start basting just before the centre. Baste to the end through the overlapped junction at **A** to stabilize the pieces, turn work round and baste the remaining part. (This action also marks the stitching line for the final seam.)

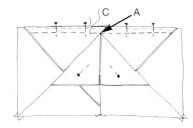

14. Pin the two halves together, matching up all the points at **A**.

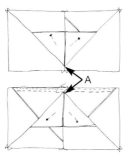

15. Sew with the basted side uppermost and follow the basting line. Sew through **A** – the S/A should be 1cm (⅜in) but may need adjusting. It is more important to sew through **A** than sew a 1cm (⅜in) seam. An enormous button may be required if you fail to sew through **A**!

Tips for sewing through point A:
- *Try the pin trick: Line up the points at the centre and push a pin through; leave the pin upright. This holds the junction steady. Sew along the seam; note where the pin is; remove when almost upon it and sew straight past.*

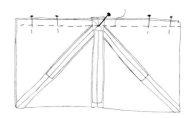

- *If preferred, start the stitching at the centre of the seam and sew to one side, flip over and complete the last part of the seam.*

- *For very thickly layered seams, it may be a wise choice to sew up to the centre (densest part), leave a gap then complete seam. Sew the missing section by hand (perish the thought!).*

- *Alternatively, use the zipper foot; set the machine needle on left of presser foot. The zipper foot passes over the somewhat thinner part of the seam (between the raw edge and the stitching line). The needle goes through **A**.*

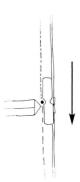

16. Remove basting, and press the last seam open and flat. Trim any excess bulk from inside the seam. Manipulate the pieces however you fancy.

Tip: *Again, minor glitches can be concealed with a small button or few French or Bullion Knots; major glitches require bigger buttons!*

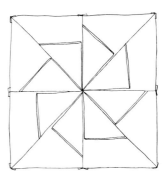

Piecing other geometric shapes

Six equilateral triangles pieced into a hexagon

Six equilateral (60°) triangles can be pieced to form a hexagon but the inserted sections may not merely touch but overlap. This might also apply to other pieced geometric forms, e.g. six equilateral triangles joined with six Trumpets (open end to centre). The Trumpets overlap.

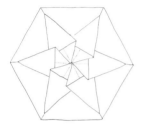

Does it matter? The design is just a little different.

Turning the insert around or setting it away from the centre could solve the problem.

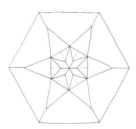

To arrange the design so that the Trumpets touch involves graph paper, protractor, compass and a steady hand. The design has to be drafted accurately with the inserts set at a specific distance from the centre. Hard sums! A 'guesstimate' with beads or (dare I say it) buttons covering any gaps may be easier, but why not turn the Trumpets round? Insert them in the seams with the open end facing the outside edge.

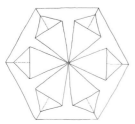

Piecing six triangles into a hexagon

1. Cut six equilateral (60°) triangles and make six textured shapes. Follow the Four Sections piecing technique (page 101) and make *three* sets of *two triangles*. Trim the 'ears' and pin one more textured shape in each seam before joining the sets together.

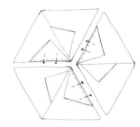

2. At the centre leave a small gap at the top of each of the three seams. (The sections have to pivot in the centre to allow the completed design to lie flat. This is sometimes called a 'Y' seam.)

Piecing eight sections into an octagon

1. Cut an octagon and divide in eight. Follow the Eight Sections piecing technique (page 103).

Tip: *A quick method to achieve an octagonal design is to cut all the corners off a square at 45°.*

As octagons tessellate with squares, how about a combination of textured blocks?

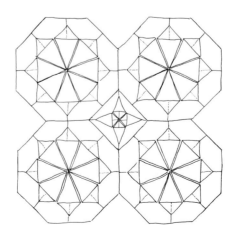

Have fun!

MACHINE QUILTING

Quilting is the securing of several layers of material. A 'textile sandwich' consisting of a top fabric, wadding/batting and a backing material is most commonly used. The layers are usually basted first then stitched together by hand or machine, although tying with a thread, string or cord, or anchoring with buttons and beads are other options. The stitching not only secures all the layers but also adds a textured dimension to the whole surface.

Machine quilting has become more popular recently. Many books, videos and articles have been written on this subject by different authors who present their own methods and tips. As with any specialist subject, it is worth reading, watching, taking classes and practising. If everything fails, there are those who will quilt your piece for you, probably on a long-arm machine.

Long-arm machines

A long-arm is a most intriguing bit of kit. There is no need for prebasting the quilt: wheels, ratchets and spindles hold the layers steady as the machine moves freely across the surface. (The machine sits on a moveable shelf or is attached to a gantry.) This procedure is completely different to quilting with a domestic machine – that remains still and the fabric is moved instead, or so one hopes!

Long-arm machines are becoming quite common in the USA. In Britain there are fewer of them, but the number is growing fast. Originally, long-arms were vast and very expensive pieces of equipment, far too large for most homes, but smaller and cheaper models are now available that are ideal for home use. Without doubt a long-arm speeds the process, and once mastered is easy to use. As I do not possess a long-arm, all my quilts and samples in this book were quilted on an ordinary domestic sewing machine.

Which presser foot to use?

Sewing across a textile sandwich with the regular presser foot may cause one of the layers to 'creep', despite reducing the pressure on the presser foot (page 9). Using the walking foot for quilting may solve the problem.

Walking foot: This particular foot has its own set of feed dogs, which work in harmony with the feed dogs on the machine. In theory, the three layers (textile sandwich) of the quilt are pulled evenly – the top by the walking foot's feed dogs, the bottom by the machine's own; the wadding is fed through as the filling in the sandwich. Most brands of walking feet are very successful and are particularly good at long straight lines of stitch. The drawback to this natty gadget is its size, and manoeuvring a large quilt around under the foot is quite hard work.

Darning foot: An alternative presser foot and the one that I favour (because it is much easier to turn the quilt) is the darning foot, sometimes called a hopper, free-embroidery or a free-motion quilting foot.

When the foot is attached to the machine, there is a small gap between the base of the darning foot and the throat plate. In addition the feed dogs are lowered or covered. As there is no pressure exerted by the presser foot and the feed dogs do not pull the work through, the quilt can be manoeuvred in any direction, i.e. sewn forwards, backwards and sideways. Indeed one can now work 'freely', wandering at random in any direction in a defined or abstract pattern.

There is a wide selection of darning feet available these days in a variety of sizes, with or without an open toe (cut-away section in the front). It is worth seeking advice from your machine store before you purchase one.

Which way to quilt?

There are several different methods for machine quilting. Here are three of them.

'Stitch in the Ditch'

The 'ditch' is the stitched join (groove) between the pieces. The idea is to stay in this groove and not deviate!

Match the thread to one of the fabric colours or use an invisible thread (nylon filament) when working on a multicoloured sample.

Place your hands lightly either side of the relevant seam to keep the work flat, and maintain a moderate even speed. (Many modern machines have an adjustable speed control – running the motor at half-speed may be advantageous. Other models cannot be operated this way; it's all or nothing and that makes it very hard to control – a good excuse for inadvertent deviations in the stitching line!)

Set a longer stitch length than usual (2.5–3mm). On corners and junctions, lower the needle into the seam through all the layers, raise the presser foot and pivot the work round. (Some machines have rather large presser feet, and these may obscure the seam – another good excuse for deviating from the chosen path!)

Finally, for those who wear bi- or varifocal spectacles, try tilting the machine (page 13) and/or donning reading glasses. This may make the 'ditch' more visible.

Topstitching or Echo Quilting

Follow the outline of a shape or pattern with the edge of the presser foot so that a line of stitch is formed around the design. Moving the needle further from or nearer to the presser foot edge will change the width of the margin allowed. As described in 'Stitch in the Ditch', use a longer stitch length, drop the needle into the work at the corners and pivot round.

A contrasting thread will add a decorative embellishment to the finished work. For those lacking in confidence, a matching thread to the fabric is a better choice – odd meanderings in the stitched line will be less obvious.

For more ornamentation, use a twin needle and two different coloured threads; fine parallel lines in contrasting colours are most attractive. Add a touch of zigzag by adjusting the stitch width.

Tip: *Do not adjust the width by more than half the maximum, or one of the twin needles will hit the presser foot and break.*

Stitching in the ditch with a walking foot.

Free-motion machine quilting

This is normally executed by attaching the darning/hopper foot and lowering or covering the feed dogs. Some sewing machines do not have a darning foot, but there may be a lever or knob that controls the amount of pressure on the presser foot (see your instruction book). By reducing the pressure to zero and using the ordinary presser foot, it is just about possible to free-motion quilt.

This subject has been mentioned in my previous books, and there is no doubt that practice makes perfect (one hopes!). This is one of those techniques that needs a relaxed operator.

Push the sewing machine further away than normal. Sit comfortably; lean towards the machine keeping the spine straight, pushing your bottom out and resting your elbows on the table to take the weight. The wrists need to be free and flexible. Relax and drop your shoulders: students with rigid shoulders up under their ears do not perform anything like as well.

A common free-motion pattern is a series of rounded squiggles (as shown in many of the photographs in this book). These should not cross over each other nor have points or spikes, but flow evenly over the selected area.

Grasp the material firmly; do not have your hands flat. Bring the lower thread to the top surface to prevent it tangling underneath, hold both ends and do several small stitches in the same place. Trim the thread ends. Maintain an even speed as you swing the work in a series of arcs (similar to steering a car). *Relax!* It is difficult at first but keep experimenting and, if you can't achieve the random curves, have spikes!

The biggest problem with free-motion machine quilting is the grasping of the work – you really need a steering wheel or something to hang on to. A variety of plastic horseshoe-shaped hoops with small handles are now available. These sit on the top of the quilt and give you something to grasp – the hoop is moved as you complete each section. Years before these came out, I used (and still do) the inner ring of a 20cm (8in) embroidery hoop.

This is placed *underneath* the quilt (between quilt and machine bed) creating a 'steering wheel' (it is not attached to the quilt).

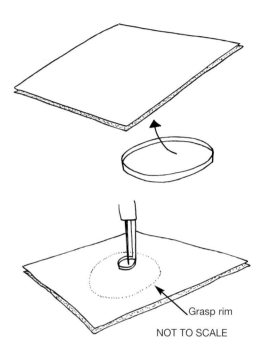

Grasp rim

NOT TO SCALE

Keep a little tension on the quilt by spreading it firmly over the hoop; grasp the rim through the layers and manoeuvre the work as you sew. Once a section is completed, simply shunt the hoop along underneath to the next area and continue. This sounds totally batty but it works perfectly – try it and see.

Admittedly, the plastic horseshoes have large handles, which may prove more convenient for those with not-so-nimble hands. In addition, some people recommend the use of special quilting gloves with raised bubbles on the front or the little rubber thimblettes (used for collating paper or counting money) to help one to grip the quilt.

Tip: *On completion of any quilting, remember to sew round the entire outer edges to anchor the layers together.*

Design ideas for free-motion quilting

- Random curves and simple continuous designs are reasonably easy to produce freehand.

- Lightly drawn lines or masking tape adhered to the material are good ideas when trying to keep parallel lines of stitching straight (do not sew through the tape!).

- For a simple quilted (albeit time-consuming) pattern, create a cross-hatched grid in any square or rectangular seamed area. This can be completed with one continuous line by stitching along the seams at the ends of the rows.

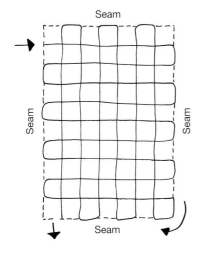

The following sketches show the range of continuous line styles that are used in most of my quilts.

Experiment, explore and play. If the design is not as intended – why worry? You are the artist and it is your own special style.

PROJECTS

Landscape Lattice Windows
50 × 50cm (20 × 20in)
Crossed-Over Tucks block with a microwave dyed and painted picture inserted. Free-motion machine quilting.
Jennie Rayment

Four original designs for small quilts or hangings are presented containing lots of twiddling, fiddling, manipulating and manoeuvring – play on…

- Read through all the instructions beforehand – I have assumed (fingers crossed) that you have read the relevant chapters.

- Pre-wash, starch if needed and press all fabrics before cutting.

- Select metric or imperial measurements – do not mix.

Tarantella

Finished size: 68 × 68cm (27 × 27in)

This is a delectable combination of Inserted and Interlocked Squares with lots of textural creativity. Good fabric choices are hand-dyes, plain-coloured materials or small, unobtrusive printed patterns.

Total fabric requirements: 110cm (44in) wide
Purple: 50cm (½yd)
Cream: 90cm (⅞yd)
Turquoise: 50cm (½yd)
Pink: 40cm (⅜yd)
Green: including binding: 50cm (½yd)
Wadding (batting) and backing material: 70cm (28in) square

Centre block

Finished size: 30cm (12in)
Seam allowance: 1cm (⅜in)

Purple: eight 16cm (6¼in) squares
Cream: four 18.5cm (7½in) squares. Cut in half diagonally forming eight triangles
Turquoise inserts: eight 7.5cm (3in) squares

1. Construct an Eight Inserted Squares block (page 77) using the purple squares and the cream triangles. Arrange in diamonds and then press them.

2. Fold all eight turquoise squares into Sharon Squares (page 51). Tuck these under edges of the diamonds and stitch in place. Sew along the

Tarantella
68 × 68cm (27 × 27in)
Eight Inserted Squares with Sharon Square inserts. An Interlocked Square border with folded squares on the corners. Microwave dyed fabrics. Machine pieced and free-motion machine quilted.
Jennie Rayment

sides of the Sharon Square and a short section of the diamonds (see photograph) to hold the shape in place, and cover the raw ends when the sides of the diamond are manipulated.

3. Roll the edges of the diamonds. Sew all folds in place.

Interlocked squares border
Finished width: 15cm (6in)
Seam allowance: 1cm (⅜in)

Cream: Twenty 17cm (6¾in) squares
Turquoise: Eight 17cm (6¾in) squares
Green: Eight 17cm (6¾in) squares
Purple and Pink: Two 18.5cm (7½in) squares of each colour. Cut all four squares in half diagonally, forming eight triangles.
Pink inserts: Eight 7.5cm (3in) squares

1. Make four *clockwise* blocks (page 55). Arrange the colours in this order:
    cream, green, cream, turquoise.

2. Construct four more blocks using the same order of colours but rotate these *anticlockwise* (page 56). Label each set to avoid confusion.

3. Sew the purple and pink triangles together, making four squares. Trim the seam then fold on seam R/S out. Baste to the remaining four cream background squares (purple side up).

4. Join all the sections in strips and attach to the central block. Press the seams open and flat where possible.

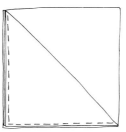

Second border
Pink: Two strips 6 × 62cm (2¼ × 24⅜in) and two strips 6 × 70cm (2½ × 27½in)

1. Sew the two shorter strips to the opposite sides of the panel and open out.

2. Attach the last two strips to the remaining sides of the panel.

Now for playtime!
1. As described on page 55, roll back the edges of the Interlocked Squares; place the remaining pink 7.5cm (3in) squares under the holes and secure all the layers with a few stitches.

2. In addition, roll back the seamed edge on the corner sections and sew down.

Completing Tarantella
1. Press the panel carefully. Lay on the wadding and backing fabric. Baste the layers well. Quilt or tie the layers together in relevant places. Add buttons or beads for extra embellishment.

2. Finally, cut 4cm (1½in) strips of green for the binding.

Coming up Trumps
*68 × 68cm (27 × 27in)
Novel Variation Trumpets
with Baltimore Rosebud
inserts. Framed with tucks
and completed with a Bias
Strip Border and Trumpet
corners. Created from
medium-weight calico. Free-
motion machine quilting.
Jennie Rayment*

Coming up Trumps

Finished size: 68 × 68cm (27 × 27in)

Nip, tuck, twiddle and fiddle Novel Variation
Trumpets, Tucks and Bias Strips to form this
delightful hanging or small quilt. It is classically
elegant in calico (muslin in USA) or, for a subtly
different coloured version, see page 96.

Total fabric requirements: 110cm (44in) wide
Calico (medium-weight): 110cm (1¼yd)
Wadding (batting) and backing material:
70cm (27½in) square

Centre block
Finished size: 30cm (12in)

Trumpets: four 17cm (6¾in) squares
Background: four 17cm (6¾in) squares
Baltimore Rosebuds: four 5 × 8cm (2 × 3in)
rectangles

1. Make four Novel Variation Trumpets as
   described on page 71. Follow the piecing
   instructions on page 101 and complete the
   centre block.

2. Manipulate the Trumpets and insert the
   Baltimore Rosebuds.

First border
1. Cut four 32 × 19.5cm (12¾ × 7½in) strips

2. Cut four 10.5cm (4in) squares

3. Mark both ends and the centre of all four
   strips as shown – 3.5cm (1¼in) from one
   side and five further marks at 2.5cm (1in)
   intervals.

4. Make one 0.75cm (¼in) Tuck on each set of marks – six tucks in total. Press all the tucks in one direction.

5. Trim the strips to fit the centre block and, if necessary, trim the 10.5cm (4in) squares to fit the strips.

6. Attach the strips and squares to centre panel using a *0.75cm (¼ in)* S/A – see diagram.

Second border

Seam allowance: 0.75cm (¼ in)

1. For the **Bias Strip Borders**, cut one 40 × 110cm (16 × 44in) strip. Cut eight Bias Strips 9cm (3½in) wide from this strip.

2. Cut four 5 × 50cm (2 × 20in) strips (**straight-grain**).

3. For the **Corner Sections**, cut four 14.5cm (5¾in) squares for *Trumpets*, and four 14.5cm (5¾in) squares for the *Background*.

4. Measure the sides and take the average measurement. Make four Bias Strip borders this length (page 95, Stages 1–6). Baste the outside raw edges to prevent stretching. Leave the bias tucks unopened.

5. Make four Trumpets (page 64). Cut the four background squares diagonally in half, making triangle shapes.

6. Place one Trumpet with the single folded side 0.75cm (¼in) away from the raw edge of one background triangle (R/S up). Place another triangle on top. Sew the diagonal (bias edge) using *0.75cm (¼in)* S/A. Remove basting and press seam open. Open the Trumpets and pin flat. Make three more units.

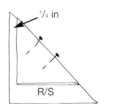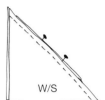

7. Attach the bias strip borders and the Trumpet squares to the panel (see diagram).

Completing coming up trumps

1. Twist the tucks and stitch down at regular intervals.

2. Divide the Bias Strip borders in sections (page 96, Stages 7–8).

3. Twiddle the Trumpets on the corners. Press the completed panel well.

4. Lay on the wadding and the backing fabric. Baste layers before commencing any quilting.

5. Cut 4cm (1½in) strips for the binding.

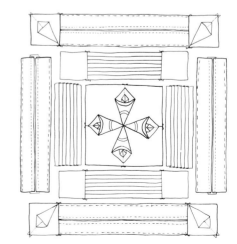

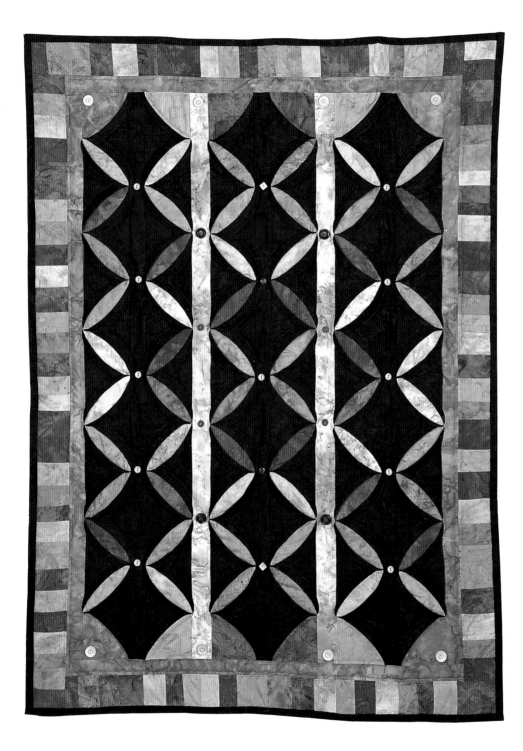

Fridge Surprise
142 × 101cm (56 × 40in)
Inserted Rectangles. Tied
with buttons and beads.
Machine quilted border.
Jennie Rayment

Fridge Surprise

Finished size: 142 × 101cm (56 × 40in)

Raid your fabric stash to create this easy design from small scraps and leftover pieces plus one big piece. Cut the squares from the scraps and the rectangles from the large piece. For more colour variation, cut the rectangles in different tints, tones and shades.

Total fabric requirements: 110cm (44in) wide
Black: 2.25m (2½yd)
Turquoise: 25cm (⅓yd)
Scraps (total amount): 2m (2⅕yd)
Wadding (batting) and backing material: 148 × 107cm (58 × 42in)

Construction
Black: Cut sixty-six 11.5 × 21.5cm (4½ × 8½in) rectangles and three 5 × 121.5cm (2 × 48½in) strips. (Join where necessary and press seams open.)
Scraps: Cut seventy-two 11.5cm (4½in) squares and two 6 × 121.5cm (2¼ × 48½in) strips. (Join where necessary and press seams open.)

1. Sew twelve squares and eleven rectangles in a long strip following page 90 – Petal Pattern Border. Make five more identical strips using the remaining pieces.

Stage Two

2. Stitch two of these strips together with one black strip in the centre. Roll back the folded edges of the central triangles and stitch in place. Make two more identical strips with the remaining pieces. (see diagram at bottom of left-hand column).

3. Sew all three sections together with the 6 × 121.5cm (2¼ × 48½in) strips in between. Add a 4.5cm (1¾in) Turquoise border to the completed panel. Roll back the remaining edges and stitch in place.

4. To make the final border, cut 9cm (3½in) lengths from the remaining scraps. Stitch all the scraps in long lines and stitch on. (The fastest way to do this is to stitch scraps in pairs then into sets of four, eight, sixteen, etc.) Check the final length carefully – sections with multiple seams stretch!

Completing Fridge Surprise

1. Press well; lay on the wadding/batting and the backing fabric. Baste layers before commencing any quilting.

2. For a speedy result, anchor all the layers with buttons, beads or quilting ties. Complete with one or two lines of stitches round the outer border.

3. Cut 4cm (1½in) strips for the binding.

Lattice Windows

Finished size: 60 × 60cm (24 × 24in)

A view for all seasons! Combine texture with Broderie Perse and shadow appliqué to make this unique wall-hanging.

Total fabric requirements: 110cm (44in) wide
Black: 1m (1⅛yd)
Net/voile: 0.25m (⅛yd)
Blue background: 0.25m (⅛yd)
Selection of **floral fabrics** with clearly defined leaves and flowers
Fabric glue/Pritt or similar adhesive (optional)
Wadding (batting) and backing material: 63cm (25in) square

Broderie Perse

An ancient art form originating in Persia, where embroidered designs from worn out ceremonial robes were saved then reattached to another garment. Nowadays, the same theory can be employed – designs are cut from one material and then transferred to another. Flowers, fruit, leaves, etc. are commonly used.

Shadow Appliqué

A piece of net, tulle, fine voile, transparent chiffon or similar is laid over cut shapes, creating a pleasing misty effect. The covering fabric protects the raw edges of the shapes from fraying.

Lattice Windows
60 × 60cm (24 × 24in)
Crossed-Over Tuck block with Broderie Perse and shadow appliqué. Tucks on outer corners held upright with a vertical bar-tack. 'Stitch in the Ditch' machine quilting.

Stage Sample showing net covering the cut motifs
Jennie Rayment

place by the net. Retain smaller pieces with a tiny amount of adhesive – a few smears in relevant places.

5. Cut twelve 11.5cm (4½in) squares of net/voile. Lay these on top of the cut designs tucking the edges of the net under the folds. Pin all the layers well.

Completing the design

1. Sew round the edges of the tucks to hold the net and floral arrangements in place. The Blind Hem stitch (page 11) is a good choice, although a straight stitch/tiny zigzag/ decorative pattern could be substituted.

2. Finally, baste the outside edge. Cut 6.5cm (2½in) strips for the border and attach. Trim the edges of the tucks flush with the border seams before mounting the panel on wadding and the backing fabric. Baste the layers together.

Finishing Lattice Windows

1. Secure the Crossed-Over Tucks lattice at each intersection with a few stitches through all the layers. Hand or machine quilt the border.

2. Add a little texture to the corners by folding the tucks together and holding upright with a bar-tack. In addition, the outer tucks around the lattice can be rolled back in arcs then stitched down.

3. Bind with 4cm (1½in) strips.

Further thoughts

● Forget the flowers and use a picture. In the photograph on page 111, a microwave-dyed and painted landscape was cut into squares and inserted in the lattice. *Remember to cut the pieces on the diagonal!* The covering net can be omitted for a clearer view of the scene.

● Think about a view into a room – a glimpse of the home, people and activities, furniture and *objets d'art* etc. Use the framework for memorabilia – insert photos, newspaper cuttings etc. (bond iron-on interfacing to the back of paper before sewing in place).

Crossed-Over Tucks panel

1. Cut one 69cm (27in) square of black fabric. On the R/S, mark all four sides at 23cm (9in) intervals. Follow the technique on page 32 but make five 2cm (¾in) tucks.

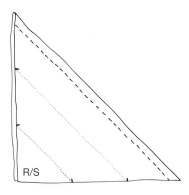

2. To keep the tucks parallel, join the marks diagonally with a very lightly drawn line. Fold on the line. Use an erasable marking pen or chalk.

3. Cut twelve 11.5cm (4½in) squares of blue fabric. Lay the squares inside the lattice, tucking the raw edges under the pressed tucks.

4. Cut a selection of flowers and leaves. Arrange in the frame. Large designs can be cut in two – one piece in one window, the other in an adjacent window. Large pieces will be held in

GALLERY

A tantalizingly textured collection of twiddled, fiddled, nipped, tucked, manipulated and manoeuvred quilts and hangings.

Magnolia Dusk
170 × 170cm (67 × 67in)
Variety of textured techniques in calico (muslin in USA) and black batik. Some samples machine applied, some samples pieced. Embellished with Floral Fantasies and Folded Fabrications. Free-motion machine quilted.
Jennie Rayment

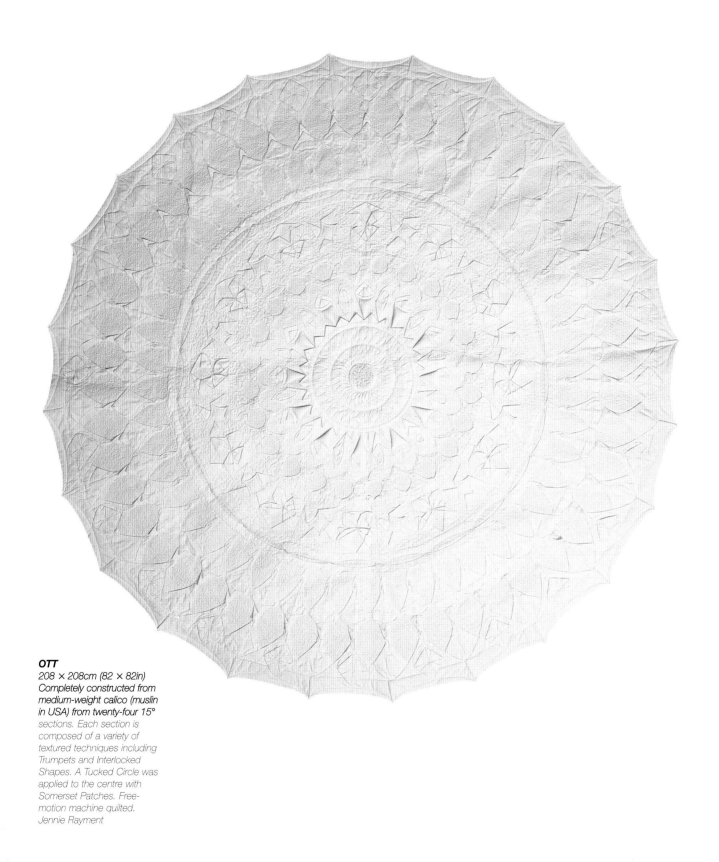

OTT
208 × 208cm (82 × 82in)
Completely constructed from
medium-weight calico (muslin
in USA) from twenty-four 15°
sections. Each section is
composed of a variety of
textured techniques including
Trumpets and Interlocked
Shapes. A Tucked Circle was
applied to the centre with
Somerset Patches. Free-
motion machine quilted.
Jennie Rayment

Mélange
122 × 221cm (48 × 87in)
Selection of calico (muslin in USA) Tucked Circles (machine applied) on batik. Bias Strip and Petal Pattern border. Embellished with Floral Fantasies. Free-motion quilted.
Jennie Rayment

Calico Creation
*78cm (31in) diameter
Sixteen 22.5° sections
joined with manipulated
Inserted Squares. A Tucked
Circle applied to the centre.
Babies in Baskets decorate
outer edge. Bias bound.
Free-motion machine
quilting.
Jennie Rayment*

All Tucked Up
*122 × 122cm (48 × 48in)
Nine panels of tucked
batiks twisted and turned in
a variety of ways. Free-
motion machine quilting.
Jennie Rayment*

East meets West
*193 × 193cm (76 × 76in)
Centre block: Novel
Variation Trumpets (squares
made from two colours)
with Baltimore Rosebuds
inserts. Other blocks feature
Inserted Triangles and
Trumpets, folded squares
with Somerset Patches.
Border of Inserted
Rectangles with Trumpets
and Novel Variation
Trumpets on corners.
Machine pieced and free-
motion machine quilted.
Donna Sawyer (USA)*

Cosmic Happening
*188 × 203cm (74 × 80in)
Experimental play with 'Take
Two Circles' (page 46).
Embellished with machine
applied textured threads.
Free-motion machine
quilting.
Jennie Rayment*

Sunflowers
178 × 194cm (70 × 76in)
Inserted Squares in a circle
with a variety of embellished
centres from applied thread
to ruching. Flower pot
constructed from
Interlocked Square blocks
and machine applied to a
tucked fabric base.
Jennie Rayment

End of the Rainbow (above)
95 × 95cm (37½ × 37½in)
Duchman's Puzzle with inserted Baltimore Rosebuds and Somerset Patches. Bordered with Petal Pattern design and Inserted Rectangles. Corner sections created from folded squares. Machine pieced and free-motion machine quilted.

In Every Direction (cushion, above left)
Inserted coloured Tucks with Origami Twist centre and corners. Pin-tucked border.

Enigma
119 × 119cm (47 × 47in)
Trumpets with Bias strip borders. Crossed-Over Tucks panels on corners with final border of Inserted Rectangles.

All items machine pieced and free-motion machine quilted.
Shelagh Jarvis

Trumpets Rule OK
155 × 155cm (61 × 61in)
Nine Trumpet blocks (four set on diagonal) with a tucked border. Embellished with Fancy Fandangos. Hoffman Bali batiks on polyester wadding. Machine pieced and free-motion quilted.
Jennie Rayment

Fishes
66 × 30cm (26 × 12in)
Tucked fabrics – twiddled to the nth degree. Padded shapes with textured voile fins. Machine embroidered and embellished. Applied to voile background.
Harriet Pelham

Finally, when all the quilts are made, use all the leftover scraps and play…

INDEX